PURCHASING BEHAVIOR
AND
PERSONAL ATTRIBUTES

PURCHASING BEHAVIOR
AND
PERSONAL ATTRIBUTES

by

William F. Massy
Stanford University

Ronald E. Frank
University of Pennsylvania

Thomas Lodahl
Cornell University

Philadelphia • University Of Pennsylvania Press

To our charming normal deviates

| Bill | Beth | Linda |
| Lauren | Clair | Andrea |

who for a time lost their fathers to a study of
personality and buying behavior.

PREFACE

This study is primarily concerned with assessing the relations between household socio-economic and personality characteristics and purchasing behavior for frequently purchased branded grocery items.

The nature of the analytical problem posed by the study required a diverse set of intellectual and methodological resources:

1. Our academic specialization spanned four areas, namely, econometrics, marketing, psychology and statistics.

2. A variety of multivariate statistical techniques, including factor, regression and discriminant analysis as well as simulation where used at different times during the course of the investigation.

Because of the nature of the problem as well as the diverse methodology used in the analysis, the study may be useful to individuals possessing a wide range of interests, such as:

1. Researchers, regardless of their institutional affiliation or area of substantive interests, who are interested in the application of multivariate statistical techniques to the study of human behavior.

2. Marketing practitioners who may be primarily interested in the nature of our findings and their implications for formulating promotional programs.

3. Behavioral scientists who are interested in how personality affects behavior.

The study was supported by the Graduate School of Business, Stanford University, under a grant from the Ford Foundation. The calculations were made at the Stanford University Computation Center. Machine time was subsidized by the Center under National Science Foundation Grant No. NSF - 9 P 948.

We wish to thank the Advertising Research Foundation for their willing cooperation in making the data available to us. A debt of gratitude is also owed the J. Walter Thompson Co. from whose panel these data originally came. Without their willingness to make the data available to the Advertising Research Foundation this study would never have been possible. A special word of thanks is due both Ingrid Kildegaard and Charles Ramond of the Advertising Research Foundation for their counsel and encouragement.

A word of thanks is also due to Professors Philip Kotler and William Wells for their excellent reviews of the manuscript. Last, but not least, we owe a debt of gratitude to our wives, June, Iris and Janice, who had to put up with the three of us for a summer during which time we virtually lived at the Stanford Computation Center.

TABLE OF CONTENTS

TABLES

TABLES (Continued)

TABLES (Continued)

TABLES (Continued)

FIGURES

I

INTRODUCTION AND
PLAN OF THE STUDY

Consumer purchasing characteristics are often used as a partial basis for market segmentation. The purpose of this report is to examine some of the empirical underpinnings of such usage, in the context of data on three frequently purchased products: coffee, tea, and beer. We shall consider the relationship of purchasing behavior, as it is recorded in the diaries of a consumer panel, to the socio-economic and personality characteristics of households. Although the results cannot be formally generalized beyond the three products chosen for analysis, we believe that they have implications for a wide variety of frequently purchased food and household items.

THE PROBLEM OF MARKET SEGMENTATION

Wendell Smith (1956) has defined the concept of market segmentation as follows:

Segmentation is based on developments on the demand side of the market and represents a rational and more precise adjustment of product and marketing effort to consumer or user requirements. In the language of the economist, segmentation is disaggregative in its effects and tends to bring about recognition of several demand schedules where only one was recognized before.

The key concept in the quotation is that there are different and presumably identifiable groups in the population, each of which tends to

1

exhibit different behavior with respect to use of the product, attitudes toward brands, and response to promotional efforts. We have found it useful to think of these differences in terms of answers to the following questions:

> What is the degree of variation in customer sensitivity to changes in the firm's promotional policies among segments? That is, do customers in one segment tend to respond to a greater or lesser degree than those in another to changes in such promotional inputs as the rate of advertising and dealing, or retail price?

The two questions relate to differences among the *average* and *marginal* properties of the demand curves for different market segments, respectively. Given knowledge of these properties, it is possible to apply elementary price theory to the problem of allocating marketing effort among the various segments.

Unfortunately, two problems stand in the way of such a simple solution to the problem of market segmentation. First, consumer groups do not come as tidy packages. There are not just a few "groups" of consumers, each exhibiting its own particular demand curve, active in the market. A model which implies that each individual consumer has his own unique set of requirements, and hence his own demand curve, would seem to come closer to the truth than one that postulates a relatively small number of homogeneous groups of consumers with all the members of a group having the same demand curve. Thus there is a problem of classifying consumers into groups or segments on the basis of their purchasing characteristics. This must be solved before the notion of "segments" can be fully defined. One approach would be to try to find groupings where the within-groups variance of demand properties is small relative to the between-groups variance. The resulting groups could then be called "market segments." Problems of identifying particular segments are beyond the scope of this monograph. They are discussed by Duhamel (1966), who has applied the theory of Markov processes and statistical factor analysis in an attempt to provide the necessary methodology.

The second problem facing those who would apply the segmentation concept is that of finding marketing strategies that can in fact be concentrated upon members of the target consumer groups. Suppose that a firm has decided to aim a promotional campaign at families who are heavy users of toothpaste—believing (rightly or wrongly) that concentration upon this group will provide greater returns than it would for average or light users in the population. Unfortunately, the firm will find that few if any promotional media cater to heavy users of toothpaste, as such. Rather, particular media attract families of various socio-economic groups at different stages of their lives and with different interests and styles of life. The specific behavioral dimension "heavy toothpaste use" must be translated into one of these more general dimensions before a media segmentation strategy can be formulated. Of course the same problem must be faced for other types of promotional vehicles.

The following list presents the major steps that are necessary to put a segmentation strategy into operation.

1. Relevant behavioral dimensions have to be identified. Management must decide whether it is interested in usage rates, patterns of preference for brands or varieties, responses to particular types of promotion, and so on. The important idea is that the dimensions identified at this stage must be appropriate to the product in question and its use environment and must be relevant to the marketing decision problems faced by the firm.

2. Given a number of relevant behavioral dimensions, it is desirable to identify operational methods for measuring the extent to which individual consumers exhibit the indicated characteristics. Examples of such measures include total amounts purchased, shares of purchases by brand or variety, and proportion of purchases made on a deal. While dimensions for segmentation that cannot be operationalized and measured can be useful in subjective types of analysis, application of any of the powerful methods of quantitative market research requires that meaningful measurements be obtained.

3. The measurement tools are applied to a representative group of consumers and the results noted. For example, indices of usage, deal-proneness, etc., might be calculated for members of a consumer panel or survey sample. This procedure allows the researcher to determine the relative numbers of people having each of the indicated characteristics and assess their potential importance for the firm's operations. It also provides the raw data for step 4.

4. In many cases it is imperative to find new variables that are correlated with the relevant purchasing behavior indicators for the sample under study. Perhaps the new variables can be more easily observed or measured when working with future samples. More commonly they provide a link between the behavioral dimensions and published statistics on the penetration patterns of marketing communication channels. The new variables serve as surrogates for the original ones where the latter are difficult to measure or where published sources do not provide direct coverage of the behavioral variables.

5. Once the identification and analysis of segments is complete, the firm is in a position to design a marketing strategy that is directed toward or will appeal to appropriate consumer types.

This monograph is primarily concerned with point four in the above outline. We seek to determine whether the items in a fairly broad battery of socio-economic (we consider this term to include demographic variables) and personality variables are correlated with some generally applicable measures of purchasing behavior.

The correlates of purchasing behavior are important because they may in many cases be used as surrogates for the original behavioral variables. Consider again the case of the toothpaste advertiser. If he desires to reach heavy toothpaste users and knows or can determine that family size and stage in life cycle are important correlates of toothpaste usage rates, he can make use of published media statistics giving reach and frequency figures for these socio-economic classes. Thus a media strategy can be devised without recourse to statistics relating media coverage directly to toothpaste usage.

The correlates of purchasing behavior may be useful in another way as well. Situations arise where it is not possible to physically direct promotional efforts to members of the target market segments. In these cases it may be desirable to broadcast the promotion to a wider audience than would be suggested by the segmentation analysis and then design the message so that the promotion will be self-selected by the relevant groups. Knowledge of the socio-economic correlates of purchasing behavior may be invaluable in designing promotional messages. Moreover, it is here that personality correlates, if any should exist, come into their own. If it were found that—other things being equal—heavy toothpaste users exhibited identifiable personality traits it might be possible to tailor the promotional message so that it would be more visible or salient to people with these traits than to the public at large.

Finally, we should note that knowledge of the personality and socio-economic correlates of consumer buying behavior may be useful in a purely scientific sense, in addition to whatever immediate practical use such knowledge can be put in the process of devising market segmentation strategies. We need to know more about the underlying structure of the purchasing process. We may also be interested in examining the behavioral implications of differences in socio-economic characteristics or personality patterns—as economists or psychologists rather than in our role as marketing scholars. The correlates of purchasing behavior can shed light on these questions, though of course statistical analyses can never provide the last word on behavioral cause-effect relations.

The needs of the scientist differ somewhat from those of the marketing practitioner—even in terms of a purely statistical study like the one reported in this monograph. The scientist imposes more stringent demands on the kind of theoretical structure that is built to provide rationales for the observed results than does the practitioner who is primarily interested in using the correlates as surrogate variables for the actual behavioral dimensions. (In the latter case attention remains centered on the behavioral dimensions, whereas in the former the socio-economic and personality variables are brought into the analysis as constructs with intrinsic scientific interest.) The scientist is often more concerned with the precise nature and validity of the statistical methods utilized in the analysis, though there appears to be no reason why the practitioner should be any less concerned about this point. Finally, the scientist is usually satisfied if he can show that there is a real relation between the two sets of variables (i.e., it is very unlikely that the statistical results are due to chance). It often does not matter if the observed relationship is rather weak, in the sense that the predictor variables provide little reduction in the variance of the dependent variable, as long as the results are clearly "significant." To the practitioner who wants to use the predictor varibles as surrogates for the actual behavioral dimensions, on the other hand the size of the correlation is usually very important indeed. A surrogate that accounts for only a few percent of the variance of the target variable is hardly a surrogate at all.

In this study we have not hesitated to shift our basis of interpretation from that of the scientist to that of the practitioner and back again, according to what appears to be the most appropriate in the particular context. For example, we devote time to discussing "significant" relationships even where it is fairly obvious that the variables under study are not related strongly enough to serve the practical needs of market segmentation.

PSYCHOLOGICAL VERSUS SOCIO-ECONOMIC SEGMENT IDENTIFIERS

The need for a contrast of the relative efficacy of socio-economic and psychological characteristics (of which personality variables are one major class) is especially important in light of the growing dissatisfaction with socio-economic characteristics as a basis for predicting the membership of customers in particular market segment groups. Several practitioners have cited the need for extending market analyses to include various psychological characteristics as a basis for identifying customer buying behavior segments. Newman (1957) presents a study conducted by McCann Erickson in which heavy and light sewers were identified, in part, on the basis of their personality characteristics. The results of the investigation were used to develop an advertising campaign for one of the agency's clients. The agency has conducted a number of studies which show that certain types of products attract customers with different personalities. The product categories studied include cigarettes, gasoline, automobiles, sanitary napkins, dentifrices and hair tonics.

The case favoring the idea that psychological characteristics should play a more prominent role in segmentation analyses is summed up in *Grey Matter* (1965):

> To most marketers "market segmentation" means cutting markets into *slices*—demographically, geographically, according to economic status, race, national origin, education, sex and other established criteria. But the idea of relating marketing strategy to *psychological* differences among customers has been slow to germinate. We call it "Psychographic Market Segmentation." . . . The *profit potential* in psychographic segmentation of markets is greater than is generally realized and those advertisers who see these opportunities clearly, and exploit them skillfully, are scoring and will score *triumphs*, while those who continue to dissipate competitive energy *only* on established notions of market segmentation may find themselves on a "me too" merry-go-round.

In spite of the relatively strong positions that have been taken in favor of segmentation based on psychological characteristics of customers: (1) there has been relatively little research published that provides an empirical basis for these conjectures; and (2) that which has been published supports the notion that where effects of psychological characteristics do exist they are relatively small.

Gottlieb (1958) found only slight differences in personality characteristics between heavy and light users of a proprietary medication. With respect to compulsiveness (one dimension of personality studied) he concluded that, "It is probably not possible to address oneself to a clearly delineated compulsive group. *What one should do is to address himself to the compulsiveness in all of us.*" Evans (1959) and Westfall (1962) report an attempt to predict customer automobile ownership based on knowledge of socio-economic and personality characteristics. Like Gottlieb, they found only a modest association between personality and customer buying behavior.

Findings of a similar nature are reported by Koponen (1960) and the Advertising Research Foundation (1964). Both studies examine the relationship of personality characteristics to customer buying behavior for various frequently purchased food products. In one analysis Koponen found that only 13 percent of the variance in total household consumption for a particular product could be explained on the basis of household socio-economic and personality characteristics. In still another product class he could only explain 6 percent of the variance in total household purchases.

The ARF study was based on household purchases of one-ply and two-ply toilet tissue. Their results were similar to Koponen's in that they were only able to explain 12 and 6 percent of the variance in household consumption of the two types of tissue.

Both the Koponen and ARF studies used data from the J. Walter Thompson consumer panel. Though the products differ, this was the same panel that served as the source for the data upon which our investigation was based. A description of the data is presented in the following section of this chapter.

Other researchers report similar findings for other product categories such as baking products (Ruch, 1965) and furniture, carpets, fabrics and liquors (Pessemier and Tigert, 1966).

A series of reports of the socio-economic and demographic correlates of different measures of buying behavior have also been published. These include studies of private-brand-proneness (Frank and Boyd, 1965), total consumption (Frank, Massy and Boyd, 1967), and brand loyalty (Frank, Douglas and Polli, 1967). Each of these studies reports separate analyses of the socio-economic and demographic correlates of buying behavior for each of 44 products. The multiple correlation coefficients regardless of product and/or study are seldom over .20.

Though most recent work has attempted to develop a theoretical basis for predicting patterns of buying behavior (especially with respect to brand loyalty (Sheth, 1966 and Tucker, 1964) little progress had thus far been made.

Measuring the nature and extent of the relationship between household *buying behavior* and household *socio-economic* and/or *personality* characteristics (such as has been done in the above studies) presupposes that one has developed satisfactory ways of specifying each of the three sets of variables for the purpose of analysis. To date there has been no systematic attempt to analyze alternative variable specifications as they relate to the problem of identifying different patterns of customer buying behavior. We first present a detailed analysis of the measurement of each set of variables. After appropriate measures have been worked out attention is turned to the problem of measuring their interrelationships.

The remainder of this chapter discusses the data used as a basis for this investigation, the design of the study, and the organization of the main body of the monograph.

PRELIMINARY DESCRIPTION OF DATA

The J. Walter Thompson consumer panel served as the source of the data used in this investigation. Household purchase records from July 1956 through June 1957 for three frequently purchased grocery products (beer, coffee, and tea) were included in the study. For each purchase of a given product made by a household we had a record of the month and year during which the purchase was made, the brand, the quantity, the package size, the cost of the transaction, and whether or not a deal was involved. A "deal" is defined as any special offer made to a household, such as a cents-off label or a coupon offering a discount or premium. There were a total of 230,000 purchase transactions for all three products combined, which in turn were generated from monthly diaries of approximately 5,000 households.

Socio-economic and personality information were also available for each household in the sample. The socio-economic variables included: (1) the sex, age, income, and occupation of the head of the household; (2) the level of education for both the husband and wife; (3) the ownership of home, TV, and automobiles; and (4) the geographic region and market size in which the household was located. The personality characteristics were based on the results of the Edwards Personal Preference Schedule, which was separately submitted to both the husband and wife in each household participating in the panel. Details of the method by which the test was administered and a discussion of the general personality statistics exhibited by the total sample may be found in Koponen (1957).

The Edwards test provides measures of the following personality needs: achievement, compliance, order, exhibition, autonomy, association, analysis, dependence, dominance, self-depreciation, assistance, change, endurance, heterosexuality, and aggression. A more detailed description of both the socio-economic and personality variables can be found in Chapter 4.

The analyses which are reported in this monograph are based on about 3,500 of the original 5,000 households included in the J. Walter Thompsons sample. The reduction was due to the fact that they control deck which reported the frequency with which the monthly purchase diaries (used for recording purposes) were turned in by each household was lost before we acquired the data. This was important because for an analysis like ours one should include only those households which turned in all of the monthly diaries for the period under study. The inclusion of other households could result in confounding the effect of personality and socio-economic characteristcs on buying behavior with their effect on panel reporting. This problem is especially acute when it comes to analyzing the association between household socio-economic and personality characteristics and total consumption for a given product. If households with incomplete reporting histories are included in the analysis they would be erroneously treated as having lower purchase rates than is actually the case. This might have the tendency to bias the resulting measures of association.

Given the loss of the relevant reporting control decks, we were forced to sacrifice some data in order to assure ourselves that our analysis would be relatively free of reporting bias. To do this we created a chronological record of purchases for each household based on its combined purchasing behavior for all three products. If one or more purchases were reported in a given month by a household, we could be quite sure that it turned in a diary for that month. We eliminated all of the households whose combined purchase history contained more than one month without any purchases of coffee, tea, or beer. This resulted in the elimination of about 1,500 households.

The analyses presented for each product category are based on fewer than the 3,500 households included in the study because: (1) none of the products were purchased by 100 percent of the sample; (2) some of the analyses required the deletion of households with low purchase rates (even after the adjustment for incomplete reporting); and (3) we split the sample into two parts at the initiation of the study for reasons which will be discussed in the next section of this chapter. The actual number of households included in each category, at each stage of the analysis, is reported at appropriate points in the presentation of results.

There are a number of other sources of bias that are generally associated with consumer panels. They are discussed by Boyd (1960) and in a report by the Market Research Corporation of America (1952) and hence are not included as part of this monograph.

THE DESIGN OF THE INVESTIGATION

At the start of our investigation there was no body of theory sufficiently well developed to provide a guide for specifying the nature and extent of relationships between various aspects of household buying behavior (e.g., total consumption of a product or brand loyalty) and household socio-economic and personality characteristics. In addition, we were not sure what set of measures would provide a complete but parsimonious description of each of the three sets of variables.

We did, however, have some thoughts about where to start, though we were not sure how many experiments would have to be tried before we would arrive at what, in our judgment, would be a satisfactory basis for specifying the set of interrelationships we had chosen to study. We recognized that the process of intensive experimentation with a given set of data can easily lead to erroneous interpretations. Even if a set of data is in fact uncorrelated sequences of random numbers, for example, the performance of a sufficient number of experiments using different combinations of explanatory variables will eventually lead to a statistically significant association.

In order to protect ourselves against this possibility we split our data base into two parts: (1) an "analysis sample" consisting of approximately one-third of the households in the screened sample; and (2) a "validation sample" consisting of the remaining two-thirds of the sample respondents. Households were assigned at random to each of the two groups. (A given family is in the same sample for runs on all three product classes.) Our experiments (reported in Chapters 2 through 5) were performed on the analysis sample. Once we had developed a reasonable model we provided a check as to the stability of our results by re-estimating the relationships involved using the validation sample.

This procedure provides an important form of insurance against arriving at spurious conclusions, even where the data in the analysis sample receive considerable manipulation.

Chapters 2 and 3 report the results of an intensive analysis of household buying behavior by itself, for each of the three products. This part of the study was aimed at developing a set of measures of buying behavior that would be both parsimonious and efficient. Chapter 4 presents analyses aimed at specifying household personality and socioeconomic variables. The next chapter (5) presents a series of experiments, based on the analysis sample, which are used as the basis for developing a final model of the relationship between the various measures of customer buying behavior for each product, developed in Chapters 2 and 3, and the socio-economic and personality variables as developed in Chapter 4. The series of experiments in Chapter 5 resulted in some further changes in the specification of the variables in our model. Chapter 6 reports and discusses the results from the final model as estimated separately for the validation sample.

II

THE DIMENSIONS OF
PURCHASING BEHAVIOR

What is meant by "purchasing behavior?" The two words that make up the term suggest that we should expect to deal with matters that are: first, related to buying; and second, observable, to the extent the term may be applied to self-generated reports of overt behavior. In the present research we naturally limit ourselves to the study of overt behavior based on the acquisition of frequently purchased food products---in particular, coffee, tea, and beer. This information is contained in the panel data which form the basis for our study.

Even with these constraints, however, the notion of "purchasing behavior" is not defined well enough to permit systematic analysis. A great many summary statistics may be culled from the basic panel data, and each of them has a claim to represent some aspect of the phenomenon we wish to study. The list of raw statistics used in this study, and a review of previous work involving most of them, will be presented in a later section of this chapter.

The raw statistics which are used to summarize a given family's purchasing behavior over a period of time may be classified into a number of different categories. The percentage of a family's total consumption which is devoted to its favorite brand of a product may be considered as a measure of "brand loyalty" or the total number of units of the product purchased described as "activity," for example. These summary categories represent alternative dimensions, or ways of looking at the overall notion of purchasing behavior. Brand loyalty, store loyalty, and total consumption have tended to be the major dimensions considered in the literature.

11

Dimensions that are defined in terms of a specific summary variable, like total consumption, may be perfectly acceptable for many purposes. The approach taken in this study, however, is to consider the matter of defining dimensions from the beginning in order to check the efficacy of the established measures. Several factors favored this course of action. First, little is known about the properties of the univariate dimensions mentioned above. Thus we felt that the intercorrelations between them and their stability over time and across product categories ought to be investigated. Second, the established measures do not include variables that have been found useful in recent research: this applies particularly to statistics based on the number and length of runs for the same brand or store. We feel that these statistics measure something important and that they might be related to personal attributes. Third, some of the established measures do not appear to exhaust the information implied by their own "definitions." If brand loyalty is based only on the share of purchases a family devotes to its favorite brand, for example, information on the distribution of purchases among its second, third, and subsequent brands is ignored. Yet this aspect of behavior may be a relevant dimension of what we mean by brand loyalty.

The purpose of this chapter is to examine the different dimensions that are contained in a fairly large set of variates defining different aspects of purchasing behavior. Multiple factor analysis is the principal technique to be utilized in the examination. The results are used to define the particular dimensions of purchasing behavior that will be predicted using personality and socio-economic information. In addition, we hope that they will shed light on what have been poorly illuminated aspects of purchasing behavior measurement.

PREVIOUS WORK ON THE DEVELOPMENT OF HOUSEHOLD PURCHASING STATISTICS

The following review reports the work of authors who attempted to define and measure the dimensions of brand and store loyalty on a household-by-household basis. In effect, their results set the stage for our own attempts to define reasonably complete but economical purchasing behavior variables, as reported in this and the following chapter. The review summarizes references that were published prior to the summer of 1964—the ones that were available before the beginning of this study. The review is not exhaustive; in particular, space does not permit us to deal with studies that have focused primarily on probability models for brand or store choice rather than on the development of household-specific purchasing descriptor variables.

The earliest investigation concerned with the description and analysis of raw purchase variables like those used in the present study was conducted by George A. Brown (1952-53). Brown analyzed purchase records from the *Chicago Tribune's* consumer panel for one hundred households during 1951, for each of the following nine product categories: margarine, toothpaste, coffee, all-purpose flour, shampoos, ready-to-eat cereals, headache remedies, soaps and sudsers, and concentrated orange juice.

Brown's principal interest was in determining the extent to which households were loyal to brands within the context of a particular product class. Although he tried a number of ways to measure the household purchasing dimensions for particular products (number of brands purchased and proportion of purchases accounted for by the brand purchased most frequently), the following definition presents the general principles of the approach upon which he put primary emphasis:

"Any family making five or more purchases during the year was placed in one of four basic categories depending upon the purchase pattern shown . . . :

1. Family showing undivided loyalty bought brand A in the following sequence: AAAAAA
2. Family showing divided loyalty bought brand A and B in the following sequence: ABABAB
3. Family showing unstable loyalty bought brand A and B in the following sequence: AAABBB
4. Family showing no loyalty bought brands A, B, C, E, and F in the following sequence: ABCDEF"

Though Brown's definition permits one to roughly classify groups of households, it does not provide a measure of how much more or less loyal a given household is relative to another. An additional problem arises when one tries to use Brown's measure to compare the degree of brand loyalty exhibited in different product classes. For example, the number of consecutive purchases which he required to classify a household as loyal to a particular brand is either two or three for shampoo, two for flour, three for headache remedies, and four for concentrated orange juice. Changes such as this obviously will effect any interproduct comparisons. Lastly, it seems likely that Brown's system of classification is apt to suffer from low reliability. Two researchers, both armed with his definition, are apt to array households in somewhat different ways.

Ross M. Cunningham (1955, 1956) developed and illustrated the use of a somewhat different set of "brand loyalty" measures. The major portion of his work concentrates on the analysis of data for a 66-family group from the *Tribune* panel who purchased a certain threshold quantity of each of the following product categories during the period 1951-53: toilet soap, scouring cleanser, regular coffee, canned peas, margarine, frozen orange juice, and headache tablets. His operational definitions of "brand loyalty" were based on household brand share (i.e., the proportion of purchases that a household devoted to a particular brand during a given period of time). The measures were defined as follows:

1. Single brand loyalty: The proportion of total household purchases represented by the leading single brand used by the household.
2. Dual brand loyalty: The proportion of total household purchases represented by the two leading single brands used by a given household.
3. Triple brand loyalty: The proportion of total purchases represented by the three leading brands purchased by a given household.

In addition, he computed brand share measures which are identical to the first and second above except for the fact that purchases involving special price inducements or deals were excluded from the computation.

Cunningham's definitions went a long way toward mitigating the principal limitations associated with Brown's approach to the problem. They provide a somewhat better means of making household and product comparisons. In addition they bypass the problem of subjective ratings.

In the work that has been thus far discussed the principal purpose of the research was to provide a set of descriptive statistics with respect to selected aspects of buying behavior for frequently purchased food and household items. The work of Brown and Cunningham served to provide a map of this previously uncharted territory and has helped to stimulate interest in this area of investigation.

Given this map, Alfred A. Kuehn (1958, 1962) and Ronald E. Frank (1960, 1962) were ready to take the next step. They concerned themselves with explaining variations in buying behavior from household to household by means of aggregative analyses as well as with the development of meaningful household-specific purchasing statistics.[2] Kuehn's study was based on the purchases of 650 *Tribune* panel households for frozen orange juice during the period 1951-53. He found that a model equivalent to the generalized form of the Bush-Mosteller (1955) stochastic learning model appears to describe consumer brand shifting on an aggregative basis.

Frank's work was partially motivated by the implications of the Kuehn learning hypothesis. Dealing with *Tribune* data on the regular coffee purchasing behavior of 536 families for the period 1956-58, he examines the possibility that the "learning" which seems to be apparent in aggregative measures could be caused by heterogeneity of the purchase probabilities for families in the panel, given that each family really chooses brands according to a simple Bernoulli process with constant probabilities. The aspect of his work that is relevant for our purposes here involves the use of household-specific statistics that are related to the order and stationarity of individuals' purchasing processes. They include the statistics for run length, number of runs, and the standard normal deviate for assessing the departure of a brand switching process from a zero order stationary base that will be considered later in this chapter.

Frank points out that two households purchasing the same number of brands (one of the measures used by Brown) and concentrating the same share of their total purchases on the brand purchased most often (one of the measures advanced by Cunningham) could still have fundamentally different brand purchasing patterns. Consider the following purchase sequences for two different households:

1:   AAAAABBBBB

2:   AAABBABBBA

Both households made ten purchases. Both split their purchases evenly between the same two brands. However one of them made an abrupt and sudden switch while the other seems to vacillate back and forth between the two brands. If one measures the probability that a household will buy a certain brand by the relative frequency with which the household bought the brand during the period under investigation both of these households have an apparent purchase probability for brand A of 0.5. Household No. 1 appears to have a much less stable probability than No. 2. Based on the observed pattern it could well have gone from 1.0 to 0.0 half way through the purchase sequence, whereas the probability of the second household buying A may well have remained constant during the entire period.

Given a household's rate of purchasing and the share of purchases it concentrates on a particular brand, one can use the average brand run length, where a run is defined as a set of consecutive purchases of the same brand, as a measure of the extent to which a household's probability of purchasing the brand in question has remained stable. A long average run length (given a household's total consumption rate and brand purchase probability) suggests that the underlying probability is relatively unstable. Frank used this statistic (average run length) as one basis for characterizing the brand purchasing patterns for individual households. In addition, he did some exploratory work with respect to the distribution of the underlying purchase probabilities across households and their stability from year to year.

He also used statistical run theory as a basis for contrasting the actual number of runs generated by a household with the expected number given the household's consumption rate and relative brand purchase frequencies. The purpose of the measure is essentially the same as that for the average run length measure described above.

Cunningham (1961) broadened the spectrum of analysis by focusing upon store as opposed to brand loyalty. Using the same measures he had developed earlier for brands, Cunningham performed a detailed analysis of the store loyalties of fifty families, based on the purchases they made for seven product categories during 1956. The products were: canned corn, canned fruit cocktail, vegetable shortening, canned peaches, regular coffee, white bread, and margarine. Cunningham found that within the period of a year a household's store shopping habits remained relatively stable. He also found that there appeared to be no relationship between the degree of store or brand loyalty exhibited by a household and its volume of consumption.

By 1962 the number of purchasing measures which purportedly describe different dimensions of buying behavior for frequently purchased food and household items had grown rather large. Brown, Cunningham, and Frank each had developed different measures of buying behavior which could be applied to brand or store purchasing behavior. Then William T. Rice (1962) conducted an investigation of the extent to which the different statistics actually appear to measure the same underlying phenomena.

Rice generated twenty-two measures of buying behavior, which covered those used by previous researchers as well as several variants of his own. His results were based on a sample of one hundred households from the *Tribune* panel in each of five product categories: margarine, toilet soap, canned corn, fruit cocktail and tuna fish, for the year 1958. He subjected the data to a factor analysis and found that the twenty-two raw variables collapsed into seven underlying dimensions. Two sets of three factors each could be used to describe brand and store loyalty. The three factors were the same in both cases, namely household share of purchase loyalty, run length loyalty, and run distribution loyalty. Rice's run distribution factor was closely associated with the proportion of runs that are longer than one purchase in length. His seventh factor was a measure of activity which included such raw variables as the number of shopping trips and the number of units purchased.

The factor analyses reported in this chapter represent an extension of Rice's fundamental idea that sets of correlated purchasing statistics can be combined into meaningful summary variates.

THE RAW PURCHASING VARIABLES

Before embarking on our analysis of purchasing behavior, it is necessary to define the raw variables that are used to summarize the information contained in the family-by-family purchase records reported by the panel. The statistics are based on the following data that are included in each purchase record:

1. The serial number of the family reporting the purchase.
2. The month and year in which the purchase was made.
3. The day of the month on which the purchase was made. (Day of month was punched only on the cards containing the beer pur-

chase records. There is a presumption that the cards were arranged in chronological order within months for the other two products as well, and the data decks were handled so as to maintain this integrity. The hypothesis that the days have been inadvertently randomized will be considered and rejected in Chapter 3.)

4. The code number for the brand purchased.
5. The code number of the store at which the purchase was made.
6. The code number of any special deal which may have been reported in connection with the purchase.
7. The size of the purchase, in some convenient units of product (e.g., pounds or ounces).
8. The total cost of the purchase.

In addition, the purchase records show the particular subtype of product that was purchased on the indicated shopping trip. The present analysis is based on regular coffee (not instant), bag and leaf tea (not instant), and beer (not ale).

Measures based on this raw purchase information fall into three classes. There are statistics showing how much of a certain type of activity the family engaged in during the sample period. Second, the proportion of one kind of activity to another may be considered. Third, the order in which various events occur may be important. The group of twenty-nine such statistics discussed in the following paragraphs was obtained by using the Household Purchasing Characteristics Generation System computer programs reported by Frank and Massy (1965).

DEFINITIONS.

Table 2-1 gives the names of the variables used in the study, classified by type of measure. Each has been assigned a six-digit neumonic identification code to aid in the interpretation of results; these codes are given in the first column of the table.

Part A of the table needs little explanation. The units in which the products were measured were defined on the basis of convenience and computer format considerations. A trip is defined as an occasion when at least one unit of the product in question is purchased. Every card in the panel purchase data file represents one, and only one, trip. Brands were separately coded in almost all cases. Stores are coded separately as to major and some minor chains, but not in terms of which store in a given chain was patronized. That is, the record may show that the purchase occurred in an A & P store, but it does not distinguish between the separate outlets for the chain.

The statistics based on ratios are also straightforward. The average number of units purchased per trip is a measure of either "lumpiness" of purchases, total consumption, or a combination of both. The propor-

Table 2-1
NAMES OF THE RAW VARIABLES USED TO DESCRIBE PURCHASING BEHAVIOR

A. Statistics based on simple aggregation

UNITS (3)*   Number of units of the product
                  purchased.**

UNIDE (4)   Number of units of the product
                  purchased on some kind of deal.

TRIPS (5)   Number of shopping trips on which the
                  product was purchased.

BRAND (1)   Number of different brands purchased.

STORE (6)   Number of different stores at which
                  the product was purchased.

B. Statistics based on ratios of different kinds of activity

UNPTP (2)   Average number of units of the product
                  purchased on one shopping trip.

SH1LB (21)   Proportion of the units of the product
                  devoted to the favorite brand.

SH2LB (24)   Proportion of the units of the product
                  for the second brand.

SH3LB (27)   Proportion of the units of the product
                  for the third brand.

SH1LS (16)   Proportion of the units of the product
                  for the favorite store.

SH2LS (19)   Proportion of the units of the product
                  for the second store.

SH3LS (20)   Proportion of the units of the product
                  for the third store.

C. Statistics based on the order of purchases

NOBRR (7)   Number of brand runs.

NBRXD (8)   Number of brand runs greater than one
                  purchase long.

NBRG1 (9)   Number of brands runs greater than one
                  purchase long.

NOSTR (10)   Number of store runs.

NSRG1 (11)   Number of store runs greater than one
                  purchase long.

Table 2-1 (Continued)

ARLBU	(12)	Average length of brand runs, measured in units of product.
ARLXD	(13)	Average length of brand runs that were terminated by a deal, measured in units.
ARLBT	(14)	Average length of brand runs, measured in trips.
ARLST	(15)	Average length of store runs, measured in trips.
ALU1S	(17)	Average length of run for the first loyal store, as taken against all others, measured in units.
ALT1S	(18)	Average length of run for the first loyal store, measured in trips.
ALU1B	(22)	Average length of run for the first loyal brand, measured against all others, in units.
ALT1B	(23)	Average length of run for the first loyal brand, in trips.
ALU2B	(25)	Average length of run for the second loyal brand, in units.
ALT2B	(26)	Average length of run for the second loyal brand, in trips.
ALU3B	(28)	Average length of run for the third loyal brand, in units.
ALT3B	(29)	Average length of run for the third loyal brand, in trips.
SND1S	***	A standard normal deviate which compares the actual and expected number of runs, for the family's favorite store. (See text for definition.)
SND1B	***	A standard normal deviate which compares the actual and expected number of runs, for the family's favorite brand. (See text for definition.)

*Sequence numbers used in tables in Chapters 2 and 3.

**The following units were used: coffee, pounds; tea, ounces; beer, pints.

***These variables were added after the main part of the study had been completed and so do not appear in any of the tables in Chapters 2 or 3. They are discussed in Chapter 6.

tion of units of the product devoted to the first store and brand, etc., are the statistics commonly labeled as measures of primary, secondary, and tertiary brand and store loyalty.

The statistics based on runs require some interpretation. A run is defined as any consecutive sequence of purchases of the same brand at one store. That is, a run is terminated and a new one begun whenever the family changes its store or brand. The minimum length of a run is one under this definition, and the maximum is limited only by the total number of purchases made by the family. The statistics for total number of runs is determined by counting the number of switches of the relevant type made by the family. The number of runs terminated by a deal is determined by counting the number of runs for which the purchase that broke the consecutive string was made under some kind of deal. The definition for the number of runs greater than one purchase long is an obvious extension of the above.

Figures for average length of run were determined by calculating the length of each run, measured in either units or trips as desired, and averaging over the number of runs found for the family. Average run lengths for particular brands or stores (e.g., for the first loyal store), were obtained by taking the average over only those runs made up of purchases of the desired type. In general, the run length information is a measure of the stability of purchasing behavior through time. It is addressed to the question of whether families switch among brands or stores regularly, or whether they tend to stay with each selection for a period of time before going on to the next. A theoretical analysis of the expected behavior of the run statistics under different assumptions about the underlying brand switching process is provided in Chapter 3.

The two standard normal deviates (SND) provide additional summary information about families' brand and store switching processes. The SND compares the actual number of runs (r) to the expected number of runs (M) for the brand or store in question. It is defined as follows:

$$\text{SND} = \frac{r + .5 - M}{\sigma_r}$$

$$M = \frac{2n_1 n_2}{n} + 1$$

$$\sigma_r = \sqrt{\frac{2n_1 n_2 (2n_1 n_2 - n)}{n^2 (n - 1)}}$$

where n_1 is the number of purchases of the given brand (store), n_2 is the number of purchases of other brands (stores), and $n = n_1 + n_2$. If the underlying choice process is stationary and of zero order (Bernoulli) then the SND is normally distributed with zero mean and unit variance. The two SND variables were added after the major part of this study had been concluded, for reasons to be discussed in Chapter 6. Therefore, they do not appear as part of any of the analyses in this chapter or the next, or in Chapter 5.

MARGINAL DISTRIBUTIONS OF THE VARIABLES.

Tables 2-2, 2-3, and 2-4 present the means, standard deviations, and ranges of the 29 variables, for each product class. All the findings are based on only those families in the analysis sample that made a minimum of five or more purchases for the product category during the year covered by the data. Thus the families for whom next to no data were available, and for which the resulting summary statistics would be very unstable, were excluded from the analysis. The final sample sizes are somewhat smaller than we anticipated at the outset of the study, but they were deemed large enough to produce stable correlation statistics.

Comparison of the tabulated means show that the average family in the three analysis samples purchased 33 pounds of coffee, 57 ounces of tea, and 189 pints of beer. These figures exclude the families that have been deleted from the sample because they failed to meet the requirement of at least five shopping trips for the relevant product. The relations between the standard deviations and the means for this variable suggest that the volume of purchases is more stable for coffee than for either tea or beer; this finding is reasonable, given the consumption patterns for the three products. This conclusion is also borne out by the ranges for total consumption of the three products: the maximum purchase for coffee is about four times the mean, compared to values of 4.8 and 7.4 for tea and beer, respectively.

A direct comparison of the amounts of activity for the three products that were generated by the sample families is provided by the statistic for average number of trips (variable 5). The average is 21.1 for coffee, 22.8 for beer, and only 11.5 for tea. Thus the tea sample is based on a substantially smaller number of purchases for each family than is the case for either of the other two products. This fact may be expected to have a bearing on the stability of some of the other purchasing behavior variables.

The mean numbers of brands and stores utilized in the three samples are not very different, although there is some tendency for coffee purchases to be spread out among more brands than is the case for tea or beer. The tendency receives additional support from the fact that the average primary brand share for coffee is the smallest among the three

Table 2-2
MEANS, STANDARD DEVIATIONS, AND RANGES FOR 29 PURCHASING VARIABLES: COFFEE, ANALYSIS SAMPLE

Variable No.	Name	Average	Standard Deviation	Range Max	Min
1	BRAND	3.3	1.9	12.0	1.0
2	UNPTP	1.7	1.0	7.6	0.7
3	UNITS	33.0	19.9	123.0	4.0
4	UNIDE	7.8	12.1	113.0	0.0
5	TRIPS	21.1	12.8	78.0	5.0
6	STORE	1.7	0.8	5.0	1.0
7	NOBRR	7.5	6.4	37.0	1.0
8	NBRXD	5.3	4.5	27.0	1.0
9	NBRG1	3.5	2.8	20.0	1.0
10	NOSTR	3.8	4.2	27.0	1.0
11	NSRG1	2.4	2.3	20.0	1.0
12	ARLBU	10.8	15.3	123.0	1.0
13	ARLXD	9.9	13.3	87.0	0.5
14	ARLBT	6.0	8.1	50.0	1.0
15	ARLST	11.7	11.5	62.0	1.0
16	SH1LS	0.885	0.2	1.0	0.3
17	ALU1S	21.3	18.7	123.0	1.2
18	ALT1S	12.9	11.4	62.0	1.0
19	SH2LS	0.094	0.1	0.5	0.0
20	SH3LS	0.012	0.0	0.3	0.0
21	SH1LB	0.727	0.2	1.0	0.2
22	ALU1B	13.1	15.6	123.0	1.0
23	ALT1B	7.3	8.3	50.0	1.0
24	SH2LB	0.145	0.1	0.5	0.0
25	ALU2B	2.6	2.3	33.0	0.5
26	ALT2B	1.7	1.2	17.0	1.0
27	SH3LB	0.048	0.1	0.3	0.0
28	ALU3B	1.8	1.0	16.0	0.5
29	ALT3B	1.4	0.6	9.0	1.0

Sample size - 670.

Table 2-3
MEANS, STANDARD DEVIATIONS, AND RANGES
FOR 29 PURCHASING VARIABLES:
TEA, ANALYSIS SAMPLE

Variable No.	Name	Average	Standard Deviation	Range Max	Min
1	BRAND	2.6	1.3	8.0	1.0
2	UNPTP	4.2	2.1	9.5	0.1
3	UNITS	57.0	49.5	424.0	5.0
4	UNIDE	10.1	16.4	92.0	0.0
5	TRIPS	11.5	5.6	45.0	6.0
6	STORE	1.6	0.7	5.0	1.0
7	NOBRR	4.2	2.8	14.0	1.0
8	NBRXD	3.5	2.3	12.0	1.0
9	NBRG1	2.3	1.2	7.0	1.0
10	NOSTR	2.6	2.2	13.0	1.0
11	NSRG1	1.7	1.0	6.0	1.0
12	ARLBU	22.7	30.1	352.0	1.5
13	ARLXD	18.5	19.9	99.8	1.1
14	ARLBT	4.6	4.7	36.0	1.0
15	ARLST	7.1	5.2	34.0	1.0
16	SH1LS	0.874	0.2	1.0	0.3
17	ALU1S	39.8	41.6	384.0	1.7
18	ALT1S	7.8	5.1	34.0	1.0
19	SH2LS	0.117	0.1	0.5	0.0
20	SH3LS	0.012	0.0	0.3	0.0
21	SH1LB	0.740	0.2	1.0	0.2
22	ALU1B	27.9	31.9	352.0	1.8
23	ALT1B	5.4	4.8	36.0	1.0
24	SH2LB	0.162	0.1	0.5	0.0
25	ALU2B	8.2	6.6	48.0	0.6
26	ALT2B	1.7	1.0	10.0	1.0
27	SH3LB	0.47	0.1	0.3	0.0
28	ALU3B	5.1	2.6	32.0	1.0
29	ALT3B	1.2	0.3	3.0	1.0

Sample size = 404.

Table 2-4
MEANS, STANDARD DEVIATIONS, AND
RANGES FOR 29 PURCHASING
VARIABLES: BEER, ANALYSIS SAMPLE

| Variable | | | Standard | Range | |
No.	Name	Average	Deviation	Max	Min
1	BRAND	3.0	1.9	11.0	1.0
2	UNPTP	5.3	2.3	9.9	0.1
3	UNITS	189.0	192.3	908.0	9.0
4	UNIDE	n.a.	n.a.	n.a.	n.a.
5	TRIPS	22.8	25.1	178.0	5.0
6	STORE	2.1	1.0	6.0	1.0
7	NOBRR	6.3	7.9	66.0	1.0
8	NBRXD	n.a.	n.a.	n.a.	n.a.
9	NBRG1	2.9	2.5	16.0	1.0
10	NOSTR	4.6	5.2	33.0	1.0
11	NSRG1	2.8	2.5	17.0	1.0
12	ARLBU	80.0	138.6	828.0	2.6
13	ARLXD	n.a.	n.a.	n.a.	n.a.
14	ARLBT	9.3	19.4	178.0	1.0
15	ARLST	9.2	13.2	80.0	1.0
16	SH1LS	0.810	0.2	1.0	0.3
17	ALU1S	105.0	157.4	908.0	4.5
18	ALT1S	10.6	13.3	80.0	1.0
19	SH2LS	0.141	0.1	0.5	0.0
20	SH3LS	0.024	0.1	0.3	0.0
21	SH1LB	0.762	0.2	1.0	0.2
22	ALU1B	93.5	139.1	828.0	3.1
23	ALT1B	9.9	14.2	80.0	1.0
24	SH2LB	0.155	0.1	0.5	0.0
25	ALU2B	19.2	24.2	306.0	2.0
26	ALT2B	2.1	2.2	17.0	1.0
27	SH3LB	0.040	0.1	0.3	0.0
28	ALU3B	13.1	10.0	88.0	1.1
29	ALT3B	1.6	1.2	18.0	1.0

n.a. — not applicable
Sample size = 247.

product classes. Similarly, the number of stores is larger for beer than for the others, and beer has the smallest average primary store share. These relations seem to make sense in the context of known market facts about the three commodities. Coffee is subject to heavy dealing and other kinds of promotion aimed expressly at the encouragement of brand switching behavior. Beer may be purchased in a variety of retail outlets, with different outlets being frequented by different members of the family.

Examination of the averages for number of runs and average run length shows that there is no systematic tendency for these figures to fluctuate with total activity. (The apparent exception to this finding is average run length in units, but we must recall that the units in which consumption of the three products is measured are different, so direct comparisons based on units are not valid.) Nor do the patterns appear to be different for coffee and tea, as opposed to beer. While evidence based on marginal statistics is weak here, it does not suggest that the ordering of the purchases for the first two products was spurious.

Finally, we may consider the average number of units purchased under some kind of deal as a percentage of the overall average number of units purchased for each product class. This statistic is largest for coffee (24 percent, with tea second 17 percent). No deal purchases were recorded for the beer sample. Once again, these results are compatible with known facts about the type of promotion utilized for the three commodities.

CORRELATIONS AMONG THE VARIABLES.

The simple correlation coefficients for pairs of the twenty-nine coffee purchasing variables are presented in Table 2-5. Only cases where the correlation was greater than 0.3 have been included; the other figures are left out in order to improve the readability of the table. The correlations for tea and beer are not presented, but they follow the same general pattern. The differences among the three correlation matrices will be discussed later in this chapter.

Reading down the first column of the table we find that the number of brands bought by a family is highly correlated with the number of brand runs, the average run length, and the primary, secondary, and tertiary share statistics. Lesser correlations may be observed between the number of brands and the number of stores. The relation between the number of brands and total activity, measured in terms of pounds or trips, is too small to be included in the table. Since the statistics for number of brands, number of brand runs, average run length, and brand share are correlated among themselves, there is a strong presumption that they all contribute to a general dimension for purchasing behavior, which we may call brand loyalty.

Table 2-5 SIMPLE CORRELATIONS AMONG 29 PURCHASING VARIABLES: COFFEE, ANALYSIS SAMPLE

(Only correlations with absolute values greater than .3 are shown)

	1	2	3	4	5	6	7	8	9	10	11	12	13	14	15	16	17	18	19	20	21	22	23	24	25	26	27	28	29
1 BRAND	100																												
2 UNPTP		100																											
3 UNITS	33	47	100																										
4 UNIDE			44	100																									
5 TRIPS			68	36	100																								
6 STORE	38					100																							
7 NOBRR	82			42	45	32	100																						
8 NBRXD	65				37	41	79	100																					
9 NBRGI	60		37	40	61		78	64	100																				
10 NOSTR	46				72	63	54	57	47	100																			
11 NSRGI	43				34	40	51	51	54	93	100																		
12 ARLBU	-54	52	43		40		-49	-45	-40	-47	-43	100																	
13 ARLXD	-53	53	43				-48	-45	-39			95	100																
14 ARLBT	-52						-47	-42	-37			79	74	100															
15 ARLST	-34		37		50	57		-35						40	100														
16 SH1LS						-57	-76	-74	-67						53	100													
17 ALU1S		49	63	30			-54	-49	-44				55	38	77	55	100												
18 ALT1S			41	57			-51	-46	-41					42		53	76	100											
19 SH2LS	32					34				70	68					41	-54	-52	100										
20 SH3LS	27				51					52	38								42	100									
21 SH1LB	-78		63				-72	-58	-50	-32					57	-90	-58				100								
22 ALU1B	-54	56	49	60			-51	-46	-40							35	98	93		-32	60	100							
23 ALT1B	-51		31				-49	-43	-36							75	71	97		59	58	77	100						
24 SH2LB	44		33		-40					44	44						-52	-51	40		-71	-52	-51	100					
25 ALU2B					51					44	42								-51					47	100				
26 ALT2B																									74	100			
27 SH3LB	55						57					-38	-38	-37							-67	-40	-39	64			100		
28 ALU3B																										45		100	
29 ALT3B																												72	100

n = 670.

The next major dimension seems to involve the total activity of the family with respect to the purchase of coffee. The number of units bought is highly correlated with the number of trips and some, but not all, of the average run length measures. Store loyalty also seems to form a separable pattern. The number of stores in which coffee was purchased is highly correlated with the number of store runs, the average length of the store runs, and the share for the first, second, and third loyal store. This dimension is apparently much like the one for brand loyalty. One interesting facet of the table is that these two measures of loyalty are correlated to some extent: the number of brands is correlated with the number of stores to the extent of .38, and with the number of store runs with a value of .46. The number of stores shows a similar relationship to the number of brand runs. This suggests that brand and store loyalty may not be totally independent phenomena, although the interpretation of the finding needs to be checked (see Chapter 3).

Many of the other high correlations in the table were to be expected, given the definitions of the variables. The coefficients between the number of store runs and the number of store runs greater than one is 0.95, for example. Yet some of these relations come as a surprise. The correlation for number of brand runs and runs greater than one indicates that only about 60 percent of the variance of one is explained by the other—in spite of the similarity of their definitions. Finally, the number of units purchased on a deal is only moderately correlated with the total number of units purchased, which suggests the existence of either substantial differences among families with respect to their propensity to take advantage of deal offerings, differences in the availability of such offerings among geographic areas or with respect to brands, or both. It is surprising that the number of units bought on a deal is not related to the number of runs terminated by a deal. Apparently the families in the sample do not tend to switch brands as the result of deal offerings.

One other important pattern emerges from the table. The average run length for the second and third loyal brands, as measured in both units and trips, tend to be correlated with each other but not with any of the other variables. The only exception occurs in the case of average run length in units for the second loyal brand, which is correlated with the total number of units purchased and the total number of trips reported by the family. Since none of the three other variables are correlated with total activity, there is no reason to believe that there is a first order relation between this cluster and the size of the sample for each family. We will find the same pattern in all three of the factor analyses to be reported next and an interesting interpretation for it will be suggested there.

FACTOR ANALYSES OF PURCHASING STATISTICS

Inspection of the correlation matrix for the raw purchasing statistics shows clearly that the data do not include anything like twenty-nine separate dimensions of behavior. The simple correlations suggest patterns of relations, as indicated in the last section, but they do not take account of multivariate inter-connections among them. The statistical procedure known as factor analysis is designed to help unravel problems of this sort by identifying the major dimensions or "factors" that exist in a given set of intercorrelated data.

The factor-analysis procedure involves finding a way of linearly transforming the original variables into a new and smaller set of independent factors which, when multiplied together in a specified manner, will reproduce the original correlation matrix as closely as possible. The important considerations are that the technique is (1) linear, and (2) dependent solely on the simple correlation matrix. (The second condition implies the former, but we include both for emphasis.) Finally, it turns out that the initial factor analysis solution may not be acceptable from the point of view of interpreting the new variates, thus necessitating what is known as a rotation of axes. Rotation yields new factors which have the property of reproducing the original correlation matrix in exactly the same way as did the original factors. (We say that the "fit" of the factor analysis is invariant under rotation of axes.) The non-mathematical reader is referred to Frank, Kuehn, and Massy (1962, pp. 100104) for an elementary exposition of factor analysis and rotation. A comprehensive treatment of all aspects of the subject is provided by Harman (1960). The factor analyses reported in this book all employ the principal axis method to obtain the initial factor solution (this initial solution provides what are known as principal components) with rotation according to Kaiser's normal orthogonal varimax criterion (the rotated solution yields what are called varimax factors).

THE FACTOR STRUCTURE.

The matrices of simple correlations among the twenty-nine raw purchasing variables for coffee, tea, and beer were subjected to factor analyses aimed at identifying the principal dimensions of purchasing behavior for these three commodities. The three analyses yielded answers that are almost the same; the extent to which the differences that were observed are important will be discussed in a later section.

Tables 2-6, 2-7, and 2-8 present the factor loading coefficients for the first principal component and an appropriate number of varimax rotated factors. A loading coefficient is defined as the correlation between the variable and the factor in question. That is, a loading of .67 for variable X on factor Y means that the correlation coefficient between the variable X and factor Y is 0.67.

Table 2-6
FIRST PRINCIPAL COMPONENT AND FOUR VARIMAX
ROTATED FACTOR LOADINGS: COFFEE, ANALYSIS SAMPLE

Variable No.	Name	Principal Component	Varimax rotated factors 1	2	3	4
1	BRAND	-.73	-.67	-.33	.10	.31
2	UNPTP	.37	.36	.07	.48	-.20
3	UNITS	.20	.28	-.08	.52	.61
4	UNIDE	-.07	-.14	.03	.30	.39
5	TRIPS	-.05	.05	-.15	.07	.92
6	STORE	-.62	-.17	-.79	.05	-.01
7	NOBRR	-.72	-.66	-.32	.06	.53
8	NBRXD	-.67	-.53	-.40	-.03	.37
9	NBRG1	-.57	-.52	-.27	.17	.59
10	NOSTR	-.68	-.16	-.90	-.02	.23
11	NSRG1	-.62	-.14	-.84	.02	.26
12	ARLBU	.78	.89	.09	.26	.08
13	ARLXD	.76	.86	.10	.26	.06
14	ARLBT	.71	.82	.11	-.02	.27
15	ARLST	.51	.16	.63	.06	.64
16	SH1LS	.63	.14	.85	-.02	.07
17	ALU1S	.65	.36	.56	.41	.43
18	ALT1S	.50	.16	.62	.05	.69
19	SH2LS	-.59	-.13	-.80	-.02	-.06
20	SH3LS	-.41	-.11	-.52	-.01	.01
21	SH1LB	.73	.77	.23	-.18	-.12
22	ALU1B	.80	.90	.10	.30	.10
23	ALT1B	.72	.82	.12	-.03	.31
24	SH2LB	-.59	-.66	-.13	.21	.06
25	ALU2B	.10	.00	.07	.72	.01
26	ALT2B	.02	-.03	.03	.45	.14
27	SH3LB	-.53	-.57	-.15	.23	.17
28	ALU3B	.00	-.05	.00	.59	.04
29	ALT3B	-.02	-.04	.02	.40	.10

Table 2-7
FIRST PRINCIPAL COMPONENT
AND FIVE VARIMAX ROTATED FACTOR
LOADINGS: TEA, ANALYSIS SAMPLE

Variable No.	Name	Principal Component	Varimax rotated factors 1	2	3	4	5
1	BRAND	-.75	-.79	-.31	.05	-.01	-.09
2	UNPTP	.13	-.00	-.00	.17	.52	-.13
3	UNITS	.25	-.08	-.01	.11	.90	.26
4	UNIDE	-.14	-.23	-.08	.26	.17	.10
5	TRIPS	.06	-.08	-.12	.17	.19	.91
6	STORE	-.65	-.18	-.87	.00	-.02	.02
7	NOBRR	-.74	-.89	-.25	-.09	.03	.28
8	NBRXD	-.67	-.81	-.21	-.18	.26	.01
9	NBRG1	-.54	-.70	-.14	.19	.03	.32
10	NOSTR	-.65	-.22	-.87	-.04	.00	.15
11	NSRG1	-.59	-.19	-.83	.05	.01	.19
12	ARLBU	.70	.56	.09	.02	.67	.15
13	ARLXD	.68	.58	.11	.06	.52	.12
14	ARLBT	.73	.80	.07	.11	.09	.44
15	ARLST	.64	.15	.70	.15	.10	.54
16	SH1LS	.65	.12	.87	-.06	.11	.10
17	ALU1S	.57	.07	.40	.05	.81	.16
18	ALT1S	.63	.14	.66	.16	.12	.63
19	SH2LS	-.62	-.14	-.78	.07	-.13	-.10
20	SH3LS	-.35	-.06	-.52	.00	-.01	.01
21	SH1LB	.75	.77	.19	-.30	.14	.13
22	ALU1B	.69	.51	.09	.00	.76	.16
23	ALT1B	.73	.78	.06	.06	.13	.50
24	SH2LB	-.56	-.64	-.04	.32	-.12	-.15
25	ALU2B	.11	-.02	.01	.55	.45	-.06
26	ALT2B	.01	-.01	.02	.68	.00	.10
27	SH3LB	-.54	-.53	-.18	.29	-.09	-.08
28	ALU3B	-.04	-.06	-.10	.41	.19	.03
29	ALT3B	.02	-.01	.05	.33	.00	.04

Table 2-8
FIRST PRINCIPAL COMPONENT
AND FOUR VARIMAX ROTATED FACTOR
LOADINGS: BEER, ANALYSIS SAMPLE

Variable		Principal	Varimax rotated factors			
No.	Name	Component	1	2	3	4
1	BRAND	-.56	-.77	-.13	.04	-.16
2	UNPTP	.20	.19	.01	.07	.12
3	UNITS	.51	-.18	.04	.37	.72
4	UNITE	n.a.	n.a.	n.a.	n.a.	n.a.
5	TRIPS	.43	-.30	-.02	.19	.82
6	STORE	-.43	-.16	-.77	.08	.00
7	NOBRR	-.47	-.91	-.13	-.12	.11
8	NBRXD	n.a.	n.a.	n.a.	n.a.	n.a.
9	NBRG1	-.35	-.85	-.05	.06	.13
10	NOSTR	-.32	-.34	-.72	-.13	.32
11	NSRG1	-.27	-.34	-.72	-.08	.37
12	ARLBU	.76	.39	.04	.07	.77
13	ARLXD	n.a.	n.a.	n.a.	n.a.	n.a.
14	ARLBT	.68	.29	.00	.01	.78
15	ARLST	.67	-.11	.62	.26	.55
16	SH1LS	.50	.05	.81	-.08	.16
17	ALU1S	.70	-.04	.48	.34	.60
18	ALT1S	.70	-.12	.60	.25	.61
19	SH2LS	-.48	-.09	-.72	.00	-.14
20	SH3LS	-.33	-.07	-.51	.00	-.08
21	SH1LB	.64	.66	.15	-.17	.40
22	ALU1B	.78	.37	.04	.12	.79
23	ALT1B	.79	.34	.04	.11	.83
24	SH2LB	-.52	-.49	-.14	.24	-.37
25	ALU2B	.20	.03	-.12	.81	.07
26	ALT2B	.23	-.01	-.03	.77	.11
27	SH3LB	-.42	-.55	-.13	.15	-.18
28	ALU3B	.28	-.00	.06	.69	.13
29	ALT3B	.30	.00	.12	.58	.15

n.a.—not applicable

Examination of the tables shows that the factor analyses were successful in identifying meaningful dimensions of purchasing behavior. That is, each of the principal component and rotated factors can be interpreted in a natural and useful manner. The four factors given in the varimax portion of the table together account for 65 percent of the combined variances for all the variables in the case of coffee, 67 percent for tea, and 61 percent for beer. In general terms, we can say that the factor analysis accounts for about 65 percent of all the information contained in the set of twenty-nine original variables. The high correlations in the raw data are emphasized by the fact that such a high proportion of the original information can be taken into account by only four factors.

The factor structure for the three product categories is summarized in Table 2-9, which lists the first principal component and four varimax factors (five in the case of tea) together with the percentage of the variance of the original variable set that is explained by each. Labels are provided for each of the factors. The meaning of each factorial dimension is determined by considering the variables with which it is highly correlated.

The first principal component is that linear combination of the raw variables which accounts for the greatest possible portion of the original combined variance. A glance at the three tables of factor loadings shows that "1 PC" is highly correlated with members of the following sets of variables: (1) the number of brands purchased and stores visited; (2) the share of purchases for the family's first three stores and brands; and (3) the number and length of brand and store runs—for all purchases and the family's favorite brand and store, but not for the second or third brand or store. This factor is not strongly related to the activity variables such as number of units purchased or number of trips. The overall pattern of loadings for the first principal component is clear: It represents a dimension of purchasing behavior that can be labeled "overall loyalty." Tendencies toward both brand and store loyalty are combined in this single factor, which by itself accounts for between 26 and 32 percent of the combined variance, for the three product classes.

The varimax factors are also stable across product categories, with the partial exception of the activity dimension for tea, which will be discussed shortly. Rotation of the first four factors (five for tea) yields clearly separable loyalty dimensions for brands and stores. Brand loyalty ("1 VA") is loaded on number of different brands purchased, number of brand runs, average run length for brands, and the share of the first, second, and third loyal brands. The store loyalty factor ("2 VA") is loaded on nearly the same constellation of store variables. A third loyalty-type factor ("3 VA") has also been identified. Labeled "consistency," it represents a dimension of purchasing behavior that

Table 2-9 FACTOR LABELS FOR THE FIRST PRINCIPAL COMPONENT AND VARIMAX ROTATED FACTORS: COFFEE, TEA, AND BEER

Factor	Label	Factor number			Per cent of variance		
		Coffee	Tea	Beer	Coffee	Tea	Beer
LOYAL	Overall tendency for loyalty: stores and brands combine.	1 PC	1 PC	1 PC	32	31	26
BRLOY	A tendency for brand loyalty: combines primary, secondary, and tertiary brand share with number of brands and some run measures.	1 VA	1 VA	1 VA	25	22	18
STLOY	A tendency for store loyalty: combines primary, secondary, and tertiary brand share with number of stores and some run measures.	2 VA	2 VA	2 VA	19	9	15
BCONS	A tendency to be consistent with respect to purchases of the second and third loyal brands, in the sense that purchases of these brands are bunched in time rather than occurring at irregular intervals: loads on the run length variables for 2 and 3 loyal brands.	3 VA	3 VA	3 VA	8	6	10
ACTIV	The amount of activity exhibited by families with respect to the product: combines total units and total number of trips.	4 VA	*	4 VA	13	*	20
ATIVU	The amount of activity of families with respect to the product, as measured in terms of the total number of units purchased.	*	4 VA	*	*	12	*
ATIVT	The amount of activity for families with respect to the product, as measured in terms of the total number of trips on which purchases were made.	*	5 VA	*	*	9	*

Key:
*   indicates that the factor was not found to be relevant for the particular product class.
PC   denotes a principal component factor.
VA   denotes a varimax rotated factor.

has not heretofore been considered in the literature. Families with positive scores on the consistency factor are more likely to be stable in their purchasing habits in the short run. That is, when such a family decides to buy a brand other than its favorite it has a high probability of staying with that brand for the next several purchases. This finding is based on the definition of the four average-run length measures for second and third loyal brands, which are loaded positively on the factor. These variables are calculated by considering runs of two kinds: (1) purchases of the particular brand in question (in this case, either the second or the third loyal brand for the family); and (2) purchases of other brands. Long average-run lengths for the particular brand being considered indicate that transitions to this brand tend to be followed by repeat purchases of the brand. Nothing is implied about how often the family switches to the second or third loyal brand, so the measure should tend to be independent of the shares for these brands in the household. This fact is borne out by the simple correlation matrices, as well as by the results of the factor analyses. It is also interesting that although the consistency factor tends to be correlated with total consumption, as would be expected when low consumption forces small values for run length regardless of the household's underlying behavior pattern with respect to switching, the two dimensions are sufficiently independent so that they appear as separate factors. A high value for the consistency factor appears to suggest that the family is "last-purchase loyal" rather than "brand loyal," in the sense that the two terms are used by Morrison (1965 a, b).

The varimax factor for activity is the same for coffee and beer ("4 VA"), but is broken into two separate factors for tea ("4 VA" and "5 VA"). No distinction between activity measured in terms of units purchased versus number of shopping trips can be made for the first two product categories. Both the total number of units and the number of trips load highly on the activity factor. For tea, however, these two aspects of activity are cleanly separated into two factors: units purchased and number of trips. The results were checked to see if the fifth, sixth, or seventh principal components for coffee and beer tended to separate units and trips, since if this were the case the observed difference in the rotated results could have been something of an accident. None of the later principal components showed the slightest tendency to load separately on units and trips. There is a strong reason why tea should be different as far as this dimension of purchasing behavior is concerned. Tea is offered in more container sizes than are coffee or beer. (The existence of very large beer containers like half kegs can be disregarded.) If there is a tendency for families to purchase only one or two units of the product on a given shopping trip, there will be more opportunity for the number of units and trips to diverge if the list of available container sizes is large. This notion gains support from the fact that the variable "units per trip" is heavily loaded on the unit activity factor for tea, but not on the activity factor for coffee or beer. The factor analysis indicates that families who are high on total tea units purchased also tend to purchase more units per shopping trip. This relation does not hold for the other two products. In fact, units per trip is loaded on its own, separate, principal component factor in the case of coffee.

COMMUNALITIES AND SPECIFICITIES OF THE VARIABLES.

The results of the factor analyses that were given above provide information on the meaning of the factors and the proportion of the pooled variance of the sample which can be explained. Before assessing the validity of using the summary dimensions as measures of purchasing behavior, in place of the raw original variables, it is necessary to determine how the explanatory power of the factors is distributed among the raw variables. The 65 percent total power of the analysis may not be spread evenly: If any variables are not strongly loaded on any of the factors they may have to be considered independently of the factor results.

The total communality of a variable is defined as the proportion of the variance of that variable that is associated with the factors. Since the factor loadings are the correlations between the variables and the factors, and the factors are independent of each other, the communality of a variable can be calculated by adding up the squares of its loadings on all the factors. The first three columns of Table 2-10 give the communalities of the twenty-nine purchasing variables for coffee, tea, and beer.

The method of determining the communalities warrants a brief consideration at this point. The theory of factor analysis requires that an estimate of the communality of each variable be available before the factor loadings can be determined. But the communalities can only be calculated by taking the sums of squares of the loadings. An approximate method has been developed for getting around this impasse, however (see Harman, 1960, Chapter 5). First, the highest simple correlations between each variable and all the others are taken as initial estimates of the communalities. Then the correlation matrix is factored by the principal axis method and the proper number of relevant factors is determined. Third, a new set of communality estimates is obtained by summing the squares of the loadings for each row of the factor matrix, and the correlations are factored again. This process is continued until the *ex ante* and *ex post* communalities agree with each other to within a specified level of accuracy, at which point the final communality estimates are taken as fact. (No one has been able to prove that the iteration process described above must converge to the proper communalities in a finite number of steps, but the method does seem to work in practice.)

Table 2-10
ESTIMATED COMMUNALITIES, RELIABILITIES, AND SPECIFICITIES FOR 29 PURCHASING BEHAVIOR VARIABLES

Variable No.	Name	Communalities Coffee	Tea	Beer	Coffee Reliability	Specificity
1	BRAND	0.677	0.738	0.651	.76	.09
2	UNPTP	0.413	0.319	0.057	.93	.52
3	UNITS	0.738	0.911	0.704	.93	.20
4	UNIDE	0.271	0.169	n.a.	85	.58
5	TRIPS	0.885	0.934	0.814	91	.03
6	STORE	0.670	0.810	0.633	.68	.01
7	NOBRR	0.837	0.958	0.891	.79	(-)
8	NBRXD	0.591	0.819	0.891	.69	.10
9	NBRG1	0.730	0.662	0.748	.77	.05
10	NOSTR	0.906	0.846	0.768	.78	(-)
11	NSRG1	0.807	0.771	0.797	.78	(-)
12	ARLBU	0.878	0.802	0.763	.81	(-)
13	ARLXD	0.826	0.655	0.215	.78	(-)
14	ARLBT	0.762	0.881	0.701	.76	.04
15	ARLST	0.854	0.859	0.779	.81	(-)
16	SH1LS	0.763	0.804	0.695	.64	(-)
17	ALU1S	0.803	0.868	0.731	.86	.06
18	ALT1S	0.910	0.901	0.928	.83	(-)
19	SH2LS	0.670	0.678	0.552	.62	(-)
20	SH3LS	0.292	0.280	0.278	.53	.34
21	SH1LB	0.699	0.659	0.659	.69	22
22	ALU1B	0.934	0.879	0.795	.82	(-)
23	ALT1B	0.795	0.900	0.831	.79	.00
24	SH2LB	0.511	0.561	0.470	.46	(-)
25	ALU2B	0.531	0.522	0.685	.52	(-)
26	ALT2B	0.234	0.485	0.609	.53	.30
27	SH3LB	0.436	0.421	0.380	.50	.07
28	ALU3B	0.358	0.222	0.505	.49	.14
29	ALT3B	0.750	0.119	0.386	.50	.33

In the present study, the basic criterion for determining how many factors should be extracted was based on the size of the successive characteristic roots of the correlation matrix. As pointed out earlier, the roots are equal to the variances of their respective factors and so represent the explanatory power of the factors. The first principal component always has the largest root, the second the next largest, and so on. When the roots have dropped to less than one, it means that all the subsequent factors account for a smaller proportion of the pooled variance of the sample than do any of the individual variables: This provides a rational criterion for when to stop factoring.

The factor analyses for beer and tea yielded four and five roots greater than one, respectively, and these are the numbers of factors reported in the previous section. Five roots were greater than one for coffee, but the fifth principal component factor was heavily loaded only on average pounds per trip. This variable had been found to be independent of the others for tea and beer, and the fact that it was loaded on its own factor in the case of coffee indicated that it was largely orthogonal for that product as well. Therefore, the fifth principal component factor was excluded from the coffee analysis in order to make the treatment of the units per trip variable the same for all three products. Given these choices of factors, the communality iterations converged to within a tolerance of 0.01 in five, six, and four steps, respectively, for coffee, tea, and beer.

The fraction of the variance of each variable that is *not* explained by the factor analysis may be broken down further into a *specific* and an *error* component. The specific variance, or "specificity" as it is called, represents information that is unique to that variable. The error component, or "unreliability," is noise introduced through errors in measurement or random fluctuations in the behavior under study. The following equation shows how the variance of any variable may be broken down into its common, specific, and error components:

$$\text{Var}(X) = h^2 + s^2 + \text{var}(e) \ ,$$

where h^2 is defined as the communality of the variable, s^2 the specificity, and e is the error component, which is assumed to be random. Since X has been normalized prior to the factor analysis, its variance is equal to one. Therefore, the "uniqueness" of a variable may be defined as:

$$\text{uniqueness} = 1 - h^2 = s^2 + \text{var}(e)$$

Given an estimate of the communality of each variable, its specificity— or the amount of meaningful information contributed by it and it alone—may be obtained if the variance of the error term can be determined. This amounts to finding the reliability of the variable, which may be done through analysis of sampling errors or by the method to be outlined below, depending on the nature of the problem.

An effort to determine the reliability of the twenty-nine purchasing variables by means of the split-half correlation technique was made in the case of coffee. (Purchase volumes were not sufficient to permit reliability analyses for tea or beer.) The twelve months of panel data were divided into two six-month intervals, and each of the purchasing variables was evaluated separately for the two periods. Then correlation coefficients were calculated for each measure, taken with respect to each family in the sample, for the two six-month intervals. The Spearman-Brown correction for split-half reliability coefficients was applied for each variable, and the results are presented in the fourth column of Table 2-10.

The correlations between the two halves of the sample tend to be above .7, which indicates that many of the purchasing variables represent an aspect of behavior that (1) is measured with fair accuracy, and (2) is relatively stable over time, at least for periods of a year in length. While the reliability estimates are high when compared to those ordinarily obtained for measures of human behavior (in particular, psychological tests of attitude and personality), they are far from perfect. Since the proportion of the variance of each variable that is reliable, and hence meaningful, is equal to the reliability coefficient, we can see from the table that from 10 to as much as 50 percent of the variability of each measure is the result of essentially random forces. This fact has an important implication for our attempts to predict purchasing behavior by using personality and socio-economic information. The best we can hope to do is to predict the meaningful component of each variable, so the coefficient of determination (R^2) based on the prediction of individual variables cannot exceed the reliabilities of the variables. The situation should be somewhat better for factor scores. Since each factor consists of a linear combination of the separate variables, some of the error may be expected to cancel itself out in the averaging process, thus making the factor score a more reliable estimate of the relevant behavioral dimension than any of the raw scores upon which it is based. This provides another rationale for the use of factor scores in the present study. Of course these maxima for predictive efficacy are subject to further shrinkage owing to errors of reliability and validity that are built into the explanatory variables themselves. This point will be taken up in Chapter 4.

The two equations given above show that the specificity of each variable can be determined in the following manner:

$$s^2 = var(e) - h^2 = v^2 - h^2 \ ,$$

where v^2 is the reliability coefficient of the variable. The specificities for the twenty-nine coffee variables are presented in the last column of Table 2-10. They range from slightly negative or zero to just under 60 percent, which indicates that the factor analysis is uneven in its ability to summarize all the dimensions of purchasing behavior.

Five variables stand out as having particularly high specificities. They are: (1) average number of units per trip; (2) total number of units purchased under some kind of a deal; (3) the share of purchases given to the third loyal store; (4) average-run length in trips for the second loyal brand; and (5) average-run length in trips for the third loyal brand. We may conclude therefore, that, at least for coffee, these variables represent relatively independent dimensions of purchasing behavior. The first two variables clearly get at interpretable and interesting dimensions of purchasing behavior. The specific portion of "average units purchased per trip" represents families' "lumpiness" in purchasing. It may be related to tendencies toward using special care or conscious rationality in shopping for the commodity: The "careful" shopper stereotype would be expected to purchase the product in its large economy size. (The proportion of the variance of the average units per trip variable that is correlated with total consumption has been taken into account in the factor analysis and is not included in specificity.) A high level of response to deals also represents an aspect of the economy-minded shopper stereotype. It is interesting that this variable is not highly correlated with any of the other measures. (It is also possible that dealing suffers from severe reporting biases.) The other three variables have specificities in the range of only 0.30 to 0.34. They do not appear to represent particularly interesting dimensions of purchasing behavior.

The fact that some of the estimated specificities are negative is contrary to theory, but may be largely explained by the method that had to be used in estimating split-half reliability. The split-half procedure was not intended to be used on measures for which the order of occurrence of events is important, as is the case with our run statistics. The division of the sample into two separate parts doubled the influence of the "end effects" on the determination of runs. Although the nature of the mechanism is not clear, this has apparently introduced a spurious negative component into the reliability estimates. The same condition holds for the share variables: The split-half correction was not intended to be used on data that are formed by taking ratios of certain test results for the two halves of the sample. In spite of the difficulties in estimating accurate reliabilities, however, the conclusion that the factor analysis has succeeded in catching the bulk of the meaningful information contributed by most of the variables seems clear.

CORRELATIONS AMONG THE FACTORS AND SPECIFIC VARIABLES.

The preceding analysis has served to identify certain dimensions of purchasing behavior. All of them are more or less independent of one another, and all have natural and useful interpretations. Our final task in this chapter is to assess the degree of correlation that actually exists between these summary variables.

Two sets of correlations are relevant for assessing the independence of factors. First, we must consider whatever correlations exist among the vectors of factor loadings, given in Tables 2-6 through 2-8. These correlations exist despite the fact that we have attempted to isolate independent factors. The reader will recall that the principal axis procedure by which our original factor analysis solution was obtained is designed to produce orthogonal components. This is certainly true, but the orthogonality is destoyed when the varimax rotation procedure is utilized.[4] The correlations thus introduced are seldom serious—indeed, the rotation may actually improve the fit of the factor analysis by tending to find a structure with oblique axes where this is appropriate. A second source of correlation between the factors is introduced by the process of finding the factor scores for individuals in the sample. The loadings presented in Tables 2-6 through 2-8 give the factor structure (i.e., the definitions of the factors in terms of the original variables) but they do not provide enough information to calculate the values of a factorial variate for individual panel members. Since we wish to relate these variates to personal attributes it is necessary to estimate their values for all members of the sample. Harman (1960, Ch. 16) presents procedures for doing this (we used the "regression method"), but the resulting estimates of different factors are usually correlated with each other. The correlations among the factor scores are sometimes serious, but there seems to be no way around the difficulty.

The correlations among the factor loadings vectors for coffee are presented in Table 2-11. Those for the other products are roughly similar, except as noted below. The table shows that the brand and store loyalty factors are correlated to the extent of + 0.43. Likewise, consistency and activity have a + 0.36 correlation. The latter is considerably higher for coffee than for either tea or beer. The other correlations in the table are negligible.

Table 2-11

SIMPLE CORRELATIONS AMONG FOUR VARIMAX
ROTATED FACTORS: COFFEE, ANALYSIS SAMPLE

	1	2	3	4
1. Brand Loyalty	1.00			
2. Store Loyalty	.43	1.00		
3. Consistency	-.11	.09	1.00	
4. Activity	-.04	.00	.36	1.00

The correlations among the factor scores and the two raw variables with the highest specificity, which are presented in Table 2-12, are much higher than those among the factor loadings vectors. The overall loyalty measure is strongly related to the separate brand and store loyalty factors, as would be expected given their definitions. (These correlations were omitted from Table 2-11, but they would have been very large there too.) The estimates for the two separate loyalty dimensions are also related; about half the variance of one can be accounted for by the other. The only other high correlations in the table link activity with consistency and proportion of units purchased on a deal, and consistency with units per trip and the deal proportion. The transformation of "units purchased on a deal" (variable 4) to a ratio was done in an attempt to reduce the correlation between it and the activity factor, but in the event it was only partially successful. The network of correlations for the last four variables suggests that consistency can be partly explained by activity, units per trip, and proportion of units bought on a deal. (The correlations of these variables are high while their intercorrelations are low.) Once again, this result is peculiar to coffee as the correlation matrices for tea and beer indicate that consistency is nearly independent of the other variables for those product classes.

Table 2-12

SIMPLE CORRELATIONS AMONG SCORES
FOR THE FIRST PRINCIPAL COMPONENT
AND FOUR VARIMAX FACTORS, AND
TWO RAW VARIABLES: COFFEE, ANALYSIS SAMPLE

	1	2	3	4	5	6	7
1. Over-all Loyalty (1PC)	1.00						
2. Brand Loyalty (1 VA)	.96	1.00					
3. Store Loyalty (2 VA)	.89	.73	1.00				
4. Consistency (3 VA)	.24	.20	.20	1.00			
5. Activity (4 VA)	-.04	-.08	-.01	.60	1.00		
6. Units Per Trip (Raw)	.40	.43	.26	.48	-.11	1.00	
7. Deal Units/Total Units (Transformed Raw)	-.09	-.14	-.02	.46	.53	.05	1.00

n = 670

SUMMARY OF PURCHASING VARIABLE SPECIFICATIONS

The analysis reported in this chapter has led us to posit the existence of the following separable dimensions of purchasing behavior.
1. Overall tendency for loyalty toward brands and stores. (This dimension may be further broken down into brand and store loyalty.)
2. Loyalty toward brands.
3. Loyalty toward stores.

4. Activity, measured in terms of units purchased.
5. Activity, measured in terms of number of shopping trips. (The two activity measures are indistinguishable if the range of alternative package sizes for the product is small, as is the case for coffee and beer.)
6. Consistency with respect to the purchases of brands other than the family's favorite brand.
7. Lumpiness of purchasing, measured in terms of the average number of units bought per trip.
8. Propensity to purchase on deals. (This dimension is not defined if consumer dealing is not an important ingredient of promotion for the product under study.)

With the exceptions noted in connection with activity and dealing, the dimensions are well defined for all three products included in our study. Dimensions one through six appeared as highly interpretable factors in the three factor analyses. Numbers seven and eight were identified because the two relevant variables proved to have low communalities and high specificities, which indicates that they are fairly independent of the rest of the variables in the study.

The dimensions identified above are included as candidates for prediction by personal attribute measures. For the last one, the number of units purchased on a deal was transformed to be the proportion of units purchased on deals, in order to decrease its correlation with total consumption. In addition, the following six raw variables are included in the analyses reported in Chapters 5 and 6: number of trips; number of brands; share of first loyal brand; number of stores; and share of first loyal store. This was done in order to compare the predictive efficacy obtainable for factor scores with that for raw variables having roughly the same interpretation.

Additional information about the structure of the factors and their differences among products is presented in the next chapter.

NOTES

1 George Brown (1953), p. 75
2 Both Kuehn and Frank were primarily concerned with questions relating to the *structure* of the brand switching process, rather than with the development of household-specific statistics that could be related to family and personal attributes as in the present study. Kuehn dealt largely with aggregative data; that is, the proportion of households in the panel with a given purchase history that bought a certain brand on the next trial. He found that prior choices appear to affect the probability of subsequent purchases. Frank attacked the same problem through the use of disaggregative data on the purchase sequences of individual households; an approach which yields the kind of statistics with which we are concerned here as a by-product of the more basic structural analysis.
3 Recent work has suggested certain other variables that might provide sensitive measures of the stationarity and/or order of families' brand and store switching processes. For example, Morrison (1965) presents results on "brand loyal" and "last purchase loyal" models that might be extended to provide family-specific indices that could be related to personality and socio-economic factors. The same is true with respect to the

work of Howard (1965), Montgomery (1965), and Massy (1967). These results were not available for use in the present study, though some of the possibilities for future research are discussed in Chapter 7.

4 The rotation method used in this study and most other recent applications of factor analysis is Kaiser's normal orthogonal varimax criterion. The fact that this procedure introduces correlations among the factors, apparently through the effects of normalization, does not seem to have been recognized in the literature.

III

FURTHER ANALYSIS

OF PURCHASING

BEHAVIOR DIMENSIONS

Our findings so far have served to identify a set of summary variates capable of providing an economical yet reasonably complete description of families' purchasing behavior. With the exceptions noted in the last chapter, the dimensions are applicable to all three products included in this study---they certainly work well enough in each case to be used as dependent variables in regressions relating purchasing behavior to personal attributes. Before moving on to the consideration of personal attributes, however, we will consider the structure of the summary purchasing variates in more detail. The material to be presented in this chapter deals with the following questions: (1) Are there systematic differences in the factor structures for coffee, tea, and beer? (Small differences among the patterns of factor loadings may exist even though the general sense of the factors is the same for all three products.) (2) To what extent are the factor structures reliable from sample to sample? (3) How are the factor structures affected by changes in the frequency of purchase or differences in the switching process for brands or stores? (4) Does loyalty for one product carry over to another product? This material is included because we feel that the problems of defining and measuring purchasing behavior dimensions are nearly as important as are those of relating them to explanatory variables, and that once a set of measures has been proposed it is incumbent on the researcher to study its properties to the greatest possible extent. The impatient reader may skip this chapter and go on to our analysis of personal attributes without loss of continuity.

DIFFERENCES IN FACTOR STRUCTURE
AMONG PRODUCTS

The results given in the last chapter indicate that the only difference of real significance among the purchasing dimensions for the three products is that activity-units and activity-trips appear on separate factors for tea and on the same factor for coffee and beer. The rationale that we offered was that tea is available in a wider variety of container sizes than either of the other products. Differences in the intensity of consumer dealing activity in the three markets provide another obvious source of divergence among the factor structures.

Certain other differences in structure are apparent from a careful examination of the three factor loadings tables. Table 3-1 presents information on the extent and character of these differences, organized in a more readily interpretable fashion than in Tables 2-6 through 2-8. For each factor, it gives the names and loadings for the variables that: (1) are loaded to the extent of 0.3 or better on the factor for at least one of the three products; and (2) differ by at least 0.15 for any pair of products.

We will consider the principal component factor for overall loyalty first. Part *A* of the table indicates that the factor structures for coffee and tea are almost identical as far as this dimension of purchasing behavior is concerned, but that beer is different in certain systematic ways. The loadings for beer are smaller in absolute value for number of brands, number of stores, and four of the measures for number of runs. They are considerably larger than the ones for coffee and tea in the cases of total number of units purchased and the number of shopping trips on which the commodity is purchased. Our conclusion is that the "overall loyalty" dimension is less sharply defined for beer than it is for the other products. Families who are highly loyal with respect to brand and store choice for beer also tend to purchase more of the product than do the less loyal counterparts. While this stands out sharply in Table 3-1, it does not confuse the identification of the loyalty factor. The three products differ by a factor of 0.15 or more on only nine of the twenty-four statistics that are highly loaded on the first principal component, so the total amount of disagreement is only about 37 percent. In addition, the share variables, which are major components of loyalty, are highly loaded on "1 PC" for all three products.

As would be expected, the difference between coffee and beer that was noted in the last paragraph also carries over to the varimax activity factor. Part *B* of Table 3-1 shows that the beer loadings are low on number of brand runs and number of brand runs greater than

Table 3-1

COMPARISON OF DIFFERENCES IN THE FACTOR LOADINGS AMONG COFFEE, TEA, AND BEER

(Variables for which at least one product has a loading of .3 or better and which diverge by more than .15 are included in the comparisons)

A OVER-ALL LOYALTY (1 PC)

Variable		Loadings		
No.	Name	Coffee	Tea	Beer
1	BRAND	-73	-75	-56
2	UNPTP	38	13	20
3	UNITS	21	25	51
5	TRIPS	-06	-07	43
6	STORE	-62	-65	-43
7	NOBRR	-72	-74	-47
9	NBRGI	-57	-54	-35
10	NOSTR	-69	-65	-32
11	NSRGI	-63	-60	-27

Total Variables = 24
Per Cent Different = 37%

B ACTIVITY (4 VA)

Variable		Loadings		
No.	Name	Coffee	Tea	Beer
7	NOBRR	53	(*)	11
9	NBRGI	59	(*)	13
14	ARLBT	27	(*)	78
17	ALUIS	43	(*)	60
21	SHILB	-12	(*)	40
22	ALUIB	10	(*)	79
23	ALTIB	31	(*)	83
24	SH2LB	06	(*)	-37

Total Variables = 17
Per Cent Different = 47%

(*) Activity loadings for tea are not comparable with those for coffee and beer.

C BRAND LOYALTY (1 VA)

Variable		Loadings		
No.	Name	Coffee	Tea	Beer
2	UNPTP	36	-08	19
5	TRIPS	05	-08	-30
8	NBRXD	-53	-81	n.a.
9	NBRGI	-52	-70	-85
10	NOSTR	-17	-23	-34
11	NSRGI	-15	-20	-35
12	ARLBU	89	56	39
13	ARLXD	86	59	n.a.
14	ARLBT	82	81	29
17	ALUIS	.36	07	-04
22	ALUIB	91	51	37
23	ALTIB	82	79	34
24	SH2LB	-66	-64	-49

Total Variables = 16
Per Cent Different = 82%

D STORE LOYALTY (2 VA)

Variable		Loadings		
No.	Name	Coffee	Tea	Beer
1	BRANDS	-33	-32	-13
7	NOBRR	-33	-26	-13
8	NBRXD	-41	-22	n.a.

Total Variables = 12
Per Cent Different = 25%

E CONSISTENCY (3 VA)

Variable		Loadings		
No.	Name	Coffee	Tea	Beer
2	UNPTP	48	18	08
3	UNITS	52	11	37
17	ALUIS	42	05	35
22	ALUIB	31	00	12
25	ALU2B	73	55	81
26	ALT2B	46	69	77
28	ALU3B	59	41	70
29	ALT3B	40	34	59

Total Variables = 11
Per Cent Different = 73%

one, and high on several of the average run length variables. In addition, the share of beer purchases for the first loyal brand is positively related to activity, and the share for the second loyal brand is negatively loaded. These results reinforce the conclusion that beer consumption is positively related to loyalty. The loadings for the brand share variables suggest that the relation is stronger for brand than for store loyalty.

Interproduct comparisons for the varimax brand loyalty factor (Part C of Table 3-1) also tend to support the relation given above, although here the result is not as clear. The loadings for the brand average-run length statistics are much smaller for beer than for coffee or tea. On the other hand, number of trips is negatively related to brand loyalty for beer while being virtually independent of it in the other two cases. The beer loading is too small to inspire much confidence, however.

The store loyalty factor is much more consistent among product classes than that for brand loyalty, as shown in Part D of the table. The differences that do occur are confined to variables that have relatively low loadings on "2 VA" for all products. The slight tendency for the beer loadings to have especially low correlations with store loyalty on number of brands and number of brand runs is not consistent with our findings for brand loyalty, noted above. Finally, the difference between coffee and tea on the number of runs terminated by a deal statistic can be explained by the known difference in the extent of dealing in the two markets.

The consistency varimax factor is not as strong for tea as it is for coffee or beer, as shown by the loadings of average-run length for the second and third loyal brands on "4 VA" in Part E of the table. This could be due to the smaller number of purchase decisions that were available for calculating the raw measures in the case of tea. (Most families make fewer purchases of tea than coffee or beer in a given time period—given that the family purchases the product at all.) The only other important differences among the consistency loadings are that this factor is much more highly correlated with total number of units purchased and average units bought per trip in the case of coffee than for either of the other products. These relations were noted in the last chapter, but no additional reasons for their existence can be offered at this time.

RELIABILITY OF THE FACTOR STRUCTURES

Factor structures based on the number of observations used in the present study are usually very reliable, in the sense that new samples produce nearly the same sets of factor loadings. The chances of obtaining reproducable factors are further increased by the use of rotation; approximations to simple structure like those obtained from the varimax method are usually more reliable than are principal axis factors. Nevertheless, the fact that we have interpreted small differences among the factor loadings for different products made some kind of check on the reliability of the individual factor structures desirable. First, we factored the observations in the validation sample for beer, using the same procedures and criteria used for the analysis sample. The results were very close to the ones reported in Table 2-8. The differences between the factor loadings for the two beer samples tend to be an order of magnitude smaller than the observed differences between beer and coffee, reported in Table 3-1. Since the numbers of observations in the analysis samples for tea and coffee are roughly two and four times as large as that for beer, we are sure that the findings for those products are reliable as well.

Data on thirteen months of coffee purchases for a sample of 535 families from the *Chicago Tribune* consumer panel were assembled in order to provide a further test of the reliability of the factor structure for coffee.

The time period began in January of 1958 and continued for fifty-six weeks—ending just before the introduction of Folgers' coffee into the Chicago market. When these data were factored in accordance with our usual criteria, they yielded a set of loadings that were very similar to the ones reported for coffee in Table 2-6. Once again, the differences between the two coffee samples were much smaller and less systematic than the ones between coffee and beer that were discussed in the last section.

The similarity between the factor structures for coffee data from the J. Walter Thompson and *Chicago Tribune* consumer panels is especially striking because of the different composition of the two samples and the disparity between the methods of administration for the two panels. The J. Walter Thompson panel used a national sample of consumers, while the *Tribune* sample is confined to the Chicago metropolitan area. Thus there do not appear to be any strong differences among geographic areas with respect to the structure of the loyalty and activity dimensions of coffee -purchasing behavior. Second, members of the J. Walter Thompson panel reported their purchases on a monthly basis, while those in the *Tribune* sample fill out and return their purchase diaries every week. Finally, the fact that J. Walter Thompson did not punch the exact date of purchase on its reporting cards (at least not for coffee and tea) made it impossible to be sure that the cards were arranged in the correct chronological sequence prior to our analysis. The fact that the measures for number and length of brand and store runs (which are sensitive to reporting sequences) have virtually the same loadings in factor analyses on data for both panels shows that whatever inaccuracies there may be in the J. Walter Thompson coffee data, they do not have an appreciable effect on our results, at least not in comparison to *Tribune* data of known quality. Since the factor matrix for tea is roughly similar to that for coffee as far as the run measures are concerned, and since tea may be expected to have roughly the same loyalty structure as coffee, we may feel fairly confident about our tea data as well.

THE EFFECT OF ALTERNATIVE SWITCHING PROCESSES ON LOYALTY STATISTICS

Differences among the loadings on the statistics for number and length of brand and store runs are important components of the total discrepancies among the factor structures for coffee, tea, and beer. Our results indicate that, in general, average run length is more highly loaded on brand loyalty for coffee and tea than for beer. Conversely, the number of brand runs is more highly correlated with brand loyalty for beer than for tea or coffee. The opposite is true with respect to the activity factor: Run length is a good measure of activity for beer while number of runs plays the same role for coffee. Our aim in this section is to examine these effects more closely and to attempt to explain the observed differences in terms of the underlying structure of the brand switching processes that seem to be operating for three product classes.

Several alternative models of brand (or store) switching behavior at the individual family level have been proposed in the literature. Most of them focus on predicting the probability that a family will purchase a given brand on a given purchase occasion, conditional upon its recent history of purchases.

The Bernoulli or zero order Markov process was considered explicitly by Frank (1960, 1962), in connection with his study of coffee-purchasing behavior. This model assumes that the probability that a family will purchase brand X on a given day is independent of its purchase history. In formal terms, the model postulates that brand choices are obtained by independent sampling from a binomial distribution, (if more than two brands are involved the distribution is multinomial). If the effects of market forces are ignored and nothing happens to upset the long run behavior pattern of the decision-making unit, the probabilities may be taken as constant from purchase to purchase. Frank's evidence indicates that the zero order model provides a reasonable approximation to the mechanism of brand choice, at least for coffee.

The assumption of independent sampling from a stationary probability distribution is relaxed in the case of first-order Markov models. (See Lipstein, 1959). Here the probability that a family will purchase a given brand on its next outing depends upon which brand it purchased last. A transition matrix, which consists of conditional probabilities for the choice of brand X, given that brand Y was just purchased, constitutes the set of parameters for the process. While these conditional probabilities may depend upon market factors, and hence fluctuate in response to changes in price, advertising, and the like, they are assumed to be independent of the outcomes of all purchase decisions prior to the last one. As in the case of the zero order model, the parameters of the Markov model are usually assumed to be constants as far as an individual family is concerned.

Finally, Kuehn (1958, 1962) presents evidence that the first-order Markov process may not be adequate to fit observed brand choice behavior for some product classes. He argues that brand choice is a learning process, and has demonstrated that a linear stochastic learning model fits aggregate data for frozen orange juice. Such a model is equivalent to a Markov process of infinitely high order, but he found that a satisfactory approximation to his data could be obtained with a process of order four.

Heterogeneity of parameter values among the different families in the panel is a problem which must be reckoned with when applying aggregate statistics to probability models of any order. The essence of Frank's argument against Kuehn's evidence in support of the learning model is that such **heterogeneity** (often called "contagion") can lead to spurious conclusions about the order of the switching process. This possibility has been investigated empirically by Massy (1965), using long sequences of coffee purchases for individual families selected from the *Tribune* panel. Morrison (1965) provides methods for dealing with herterogeneity in zero order and special Markov models, using short sequences of purchases; he also tests his results on *Tribune* coffee data.

The nature of the process which generates families' successive choices of brands or stores has important implications for the type of summary purchasing statistic which should be used to describe such behavior. If the underlying process is zero order, for example, all the information relevant for its description is summed up in the set of multinomial sampling probabilities. Since the sample relative frequencies are maximum likelihood estimators of the relevant population parameters, there is no need to supplement them with run length or other types of measure. (Of course the problem of combining the set of relative frequencies into a single measure of "brand loyalty" remains.) If the relevant process is of a first or higher-order Markov type, however, the vector of sample relative purchase frequencies is no longer sufficient to describe loyalty. Ideally, the matrix of conditional probabilities should be estimated for each family in the sample, and these parameters used to define a measure of loyalty. Unfortunately, the transition matrix cannot be estimated on a family-by-family basis when the number of purchases available for each decision making unit is small. (See Telser, (1963) for a discussion of methods that might be applicable for larger samples.) It is here that statistics for run length and number of runs become potentially important.

A SIMULATION MODEL FOR STUDYING LOYALTY STATISTICS.

Run length measures affect the dimensions of loyalty and activity differently for our three product classes. Appraisal of the results presented in the previous sections suggested that these differences might be due to either: (1) differences in the structure of brand and choice behavior with respect to the three products, as discussed above; or (2) differences in numbers and distribution of the observed purchase decisions in the three samples. As indicated in Chapter 2, for instance, the average number of shopping trips made by families in the analysis sample is largest for coffee and beer and much smaller for tea. The range of the number of trips is much greater for beer than for either coffee or tea. Differences like these could be expected to make a difference the degree to which specific run variables are associated with the various factors.

Given that the number of purchase decisions made by many families in the sample during the period covered by the data is uncomfortably small, the only possibility for empirically studying the effects of changes in sample size was to somehow *increase* the size of the sample. Since adding real data was out of the question, a simulation model was designed and run for each of the product categories. Many of the attributes of the original sample were maintained in the simulation, by methods to be discussed below. Therefore, the results of the simulation are comparable to the empirical findings reported in the previous sections.

The macro flow diagram of the simulation system is presented in Figure 3-1. All of the calculations proceed on a family-by-family basis. The first step for each family is to read that family's actual purchase history for the product being simulated from the Household Purchasing Generation System (HPCGS) output tape used as the basis for our previous results. This information forms the basis for setting up the family's purchase probability vectors. (The method by which this is done will be reported below.) The resulting information is transmitted to the purchase generation section of the simulation program. Simulated purchases are generated one at a time by drawing random numbers and comparing them with the purchase probability vectors.

The record for each simulated purchase contains the following information:
1. A code number for the brand purchased.
2. A code number for the store at which the purchase was made.
3. The number of units purchased.

The size of package purchased (i.e., a one or two-pound can in the case of coffee) was taken to be one for all purchases generated by the simulation. Since the statistic for number of units purchased is based on the average amount of product purchased per trip by the family, as taken from the actual data, this simplification does not involve a loss of

Figure 3-1
FLOW DIAGRAM OF SIMULATION SYSTEM

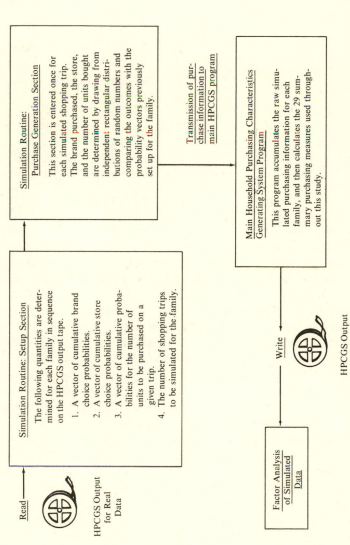

Read ──→

HPCGS Output
for Real
Data

Simulation Routine: Setup Section

The following quantities are determined for each family in sequence
on the HPCGS output tape.

1. A vector of cumulative brand
   choice probabilities.
2. A vector of cumulative store
   choice probabilities.
3. A vector of cumulative probabilities for the number of
   units to be purchased on a
   given trip.
4. The number of shopping trips
   to be simulated for the family.

Simulation Routine:
Purchase Generation Section

This section is entered once for
each simulated shopping trip.
The brand purchased, the store,
and the number of units bought
are determined by drawing from
independent rectangular distributions of random numbers and
comparing the outcomes with the
probability vectors previously
set up for the family.

Transmission of pur-
chase information to
main HPCGS program

Main Household Purchasing Characteristics
Generating System Program

This program accumulates the raw simulated purchasing information for each
family, and then calculates the 29 summary purchasing measures used through-
out this study.

Write ───

HPCGS Output
for Simulated Data.

Factor Analysis
of Simulated
Data

generality. Finally, the simulation was not designed to include dealing behavior. Therefore, the "deal" code required by HPCGS for every purchase was always set to zero (no deal present).

The probability vector for brand choice is set up by accumulating the shares for all the brands purchased by the family, as read from the HPCGS tape based on the real data. Consider a family who purchased the following brands, for example:

	A	B	C	D	E	Total
Share of units purchased	.07	.54	.21	.08	.10	1.00

The simulation is set up so that this family would have a 7 percent chance of purchasing brand A on a given trip, a 54 percent chance for brand B, and so forth. This is accomplished by putting the following vector of cumulative probabilities into the memory of the computer:

$$(\quad .07, \quad .61, \quad .82, \quad .90, \quad 1.00 \quad) \quad .$$

A random number with a rectangular distribution over the range 0-1 is generated by the computer: if this number is below .07 the purchase is assigned to brand A; if it is between .07 and .61 brand B is selected, etc. This results in the generation of a series of brand choices with approximately the same marginal probability distribution as actually governs the behavior of the particular family being simulated.

The method for specifying the probability vectors for families fails to exactly match the relevant real distributions in two respects. First, the information on family brand shares that was available from the output of the HPCGS program is based on relative total physical weight of product purchased rather than on the proportion of shopping trips devoted to each brand by the family. Yet the latter measure is the relevant one as far as the simulation is concerned. Second, the observed probability vector is only an estimate of the family's true probability vector. Where the number of purchase decisions is small, as is the case for a good many families in the sample, brands that have a small but non-zero probability of being selected may never be purchased. Thus the empirical probability estimates tend to understate the number of brands that might actually be purchased, given the underlying probability structure for the family. While the reservations are of theoretical interest, they do not appear to be serious as far as the purposes of the present analysis are concerned.

The vector of store probabilities is set up in nearly the same way as for brand choice. The only difference is due to the fact that empirical store share information is calculated by HPCGS only for the three stores that account for the largest proportions of a family's purchases.

The simulation probabilities for these three stores are handled in exactly the same way as for brands. If a family purchased the product in more than three stores (information on the number of stores shopped is available from HPCGS), the remaining share is divided equally among the extra stores. Consider a family that purchased in five stores, for example. If the three stores with the highest purchase rates account for 80 percent of the families' total activity, stores four and five would be assigned 10 percent probabilities each, for a total of 100 percent. If the same family had purchased in six stores, the three stores with the smallest activities would arbitrarily be assigned 6.7% shares. Since most families concentrate the bulk of their purchases in three or fewer stores, the degree of approximation introduced by this procedure is not serious.

The probability distribution for the number of units purchased on a given trip is determined by assuming that the size distribution of purchases is distributed according to a Poisson law. The mean number of physical units of product purchased per shopping trip is read from the HPCGS output tape. The probability that the family will purchase exactly k units on a given shopping trip is determined from a Poisson distribution with a mean of one less than the average of units per trip for the family, as shown by the following formula:

$$\Pr(\text{units} = \underline{k}) = \frac{e^{-m}m^k}{k!}$$

where m = (average units per trip for the family - 1.0). The constant is subtracted in order to exclude the possibilty that a purchase may be of size zero.

The use of a Poisson distribution for determining the size of each purchase is another approximation to actual purchasing behavior. There is some evidence that the number of purchases for individual consuming units is distributed over time in a Poisson fashion, but these models assume a constant time interval and include the possibility that there will not be any purchase during the interval (See Ehrenberg, 1959). These conditions do not quite apply to our situation, since the length of the period between purchases is variable and the statistic whose probability is being approximated is the number of units purchased, given that a purchase will occur. Nevertheless, the inspection of the empirical data suggests that the Poisson distribution is reasonably appropriate as far as the purposes of the simulation is concerned. [2]

The number of shopping trips to be simulated for each family is based on the number of trips actually reported for the product being studied, during the twelve months covered by our data. The number of simulated trips was set equal to the actual number for some runs, in order to compare the results of the simulation with those based on real data. Then the affect of sample size was explored by running the simulation with the number of trips set at three times the actual number for each family.

The simulation was easy to program for the IBM 7090, since the necessary programs for data summarization already existed as part of the HPCGS system. The simulation subroutines were merely inserted in place of the usual data reading routines of the HPCGS. The running time for the simulation was very short as well: a typical simulation run took only about one-third of the time required to run HPCGS on live data for the same number of families.

FACTOR ANALYSES OF SIMULATED PURCHASING STATISTICS.

The simulation was run for all three product categories. The present discussion will be based largely on beer, for reasons to be discussed below. The results were generally similar for the three products; where observed differences are important they will be explicitly considered.

Table 3-2 compares the means and standard deviations of the raw purchasing statistics for beer for the actual data and two simulation runs. The same families are represented in all three cases, so the results should be comparable within the limits of the design of the simulation.

The information for the number of brands purchased and stores visited, and the shares of the first, second, and third brands and stores are nearly the same for the actual data and the simulation based on three times the actual number trips (SIM X 3). There is a slight tendency for the SIM X 1 to reduce the number of brands and stores and increase the share of the first loyal brand and store, but this is to be expected since low probability choices tend not to get drawn when the number of purchases made by a given family is small. The information on total trips is controlled exactly by the simulation, and so is comparable across the three runs. (The last family on the data tape was inadvertently left out of the simulation, so the numbers differ slightly.)

The figures for total number of units purchased and average units purchased per shopping trip show that the simulation was not fully successful in approximating the probability distribution for the number of units bought on a given purchase occasion. The difficulty seems to lie in the range of large purchases. The Poisson distribution apparently produces multi-unit purchase probabilities that are too high for the majority of families in the sample, while being too low for families that consume a greater deal of beer. (The range of activity among families is much greater for beer than for either tea or coffee.) These effects are much less serious for tea and coffee, as can be seen from the following tabulation, which presents a comparison of the relevant means for the three product classes.

Table 3-2
MEANS AND STANDARD DEVIATIONS FOR ACTUAL AND SIMULATED PURCHASING STATISTICS: BEER

No.	Variable Name	Actual Sample M.	Actual Sample S.D.	Simulation (SIM X 1) M.	Simulation (SIM X 1) S.D.	Simulation (SIM X 3) M.	Simulation (SIM X 3) S.D.
1	BRAND	3.0	1.9	2.5	1.5	2.9	1.8
2	UNPTP	5.34	2.27	5.30	2.04	5.29	2.03
3	UNITS	189.0	192.3	113.7	121.6	283.5	231.1
4	UNIDE	n.a	n.a	n.a	n.a	n.a	n.a
5	TRIPS	22.8	25.1	22.2	23.3	66.7	69.9
6	STORE	2.1	1.0	1.9	0.8	2.0	0.9
7	NOBRR	6.3	7.9	7.9	10.2	22.5	31.7
8	NBRXD	n.a	n.a	n.a	n.a	n.a	n.a
9	NBRG1	2.9	2.5	3.3	3.6	8.6	11.1
10	NOSTR	4.6	5.2	6.2	8.2	16.6	23.7
11	NSRG1	2.8	2.5	3.1	3.5	7.7	10.3
12	ARLBU	80.0	138.6	44.7	82.3	88.3	169.9
13	ARLXD	n.a	n.a	n.a	n.a	n.a	n.a
14	ARLBT	9.3	19.4	8.2	16.4	20.5	50.1
15	ARLST	9.2	13.2	8.8	13.1	14.4	20.3
16	SH1LS	0.810	0.2	0.834	0.2	0.820	0.2
17	ALU1S	105.0	157.4	53.4	87.7	115.7	188.8
18	ALT1S	10.6	13.3	9.6	13.0	15.9	20.0
19	SH2LS	0.141	0.1	0.128	0.1	0.145	0.1
20	SH3LS	0.024	0.1	0.0.6	0.0	0.028	0.1
21	SH1LB	0.762	0.2	0.758	0.2	0.744	0.2
22	ALU1B	93.5	139.1	48.6	81.7	95.4	170.0
23	ALT1B	9.9	14.2	8.6	13.0	13.0	19.0
24	SH2LB	0.155	0.1	0.160	0.1	0.163	0.1
25	ALU2B	19.2	24.2	6.5	2.9	6.5	2.6
26	ALT2B	2.1	2.2	1.3	0.3	1.3	0.3
27	SH3LB	0.040	0.1	0.042	0.1	0.048	0.1
28	ALU3B	13.1	10.0	5.4	1.5	5.4	1.7
29	ALT3B	1.6	1.2	1.1	0.2	1.1	0.1
Sample Size		247		246		246	

n.a—not applicable

	Average Number of Units		Average Units Per Trip	
	Actual	SIM X 1	Actual	SIM X 1
Coffee	33	35	1.7	1.8
Tea	57	47	4.1	4.1
Beer	189	113	5.3	5.3

We shall see that the factor structure obtained from the coffee simulation, where the Poisson fit is extremely good, does not differ substantially from that for the beer simulation. The same is true for tea. Therefore, we may conclude that the method for simulating the number of units purchased per trip is acceptable.

The behavior of the run variables for beer may best be considered in terms of factor analyses of the simulation output, which are presented in Tables 3-3 and 3-4. The loadings presented in these tables should be compared with those obtained from our live data, which are given in Table 2-8. The same general factor structure emerges from the actual and both sets of simulated data. The first principal component is a generalized loyalty dimension in all cases. Although the relative importance of the varimax rotated factors differs from analysis to analysis, the same factors are always present.

The patterns of loadings differ in a number of interesting respects, as indicated by the following comparisons of the varimax factors given in the three tables.

1. The statistics for *number of brand runs* and *number of store runs* are strongly loaded on their respective loyalty factors in the case of the ACTUAL analysis. They are loaded on both loyalty and activity for SIM X 1 and strongly on activity alone in the case of SIM X 3. This is true for both total number of runs and number of runs greater than one.

2. The overall *average run length* statistics for brands and stores have relatively large loadings on both loyalty and activity in the ACTUAL case. For SIM X 3 their loadings are concentrated on loyalty. SIM X 1 falls between ACTUAL and SIM X 3. The trend for average run length is just the opposite of that for the number of runs.

3. The *average run lengths* for *first loyal store* and *first loyal brand* are most closely associated with activity for the ACTUAL data. The situation is reversed for the SIM X 1, where they are heavily loaded on the store and brand loyalty factors, respectively. The SIM X 3 yielded even higher loadings for loyalty and lower ones for activity, as far as these variables are concerned. The trend is in the same direction as the one already noted for the overall run length measures, and considerably more pronounced.

4. Units per trip is loaded much more heavily on the consistency factor in the simulation runs than for the ACTUAL data. The average run length in trips for second and third loyal brands are not as heavily loaded on consistency for SIM X 1 as for SIM X 3 or the ACTUAL data, although the meaning of the consistency factor remains clear for all three cases.

5. The *number of brands* and the *number of stores* are more heavily loaded on activity for the two simulation runs than for the ACTUAL data, although by far their heaviest loadings are on loyalty in all cases.

The differences between the loadings for the ACTUAL and SIM X 1 factor analyses suggest that brand and store choice behavior for beer does not follow a simple Bernoulli probability law, as built into the simulation model.[3]

Table 3-3
FACTOR LOADINGS FOR SIMULATED
BEER PURCHASING STATISTICS,
BASED ON ANALYSIS SAMPLE:
ACTUAL NUMBER OF TRIPS

Variable No.	Name	Principal Component	Varimax rotated factors 1	2	3	4
1	BRAND	-.75	-.69	-.17	.02	.36
2	UNPTP	.26	.28	.07	.66	-.03
3	UNITS	.12	.24	.03	.31	.83
4	UNIDE	n.a.	n.a.	n.a.	n.a.	n.a.
5	TRIPS	.06	.21	-.06	-.00	.93
6	STORE	-.35	-.08	-.77	.01	.12
7	NOBRR	-.67	-.58	-.08	.09	.74
8	NBRXD	n.a.	n.a.	n.a.	n.a.	n.a.
9	NBRG1	-.54	-.48	.02	.10	.74
10	NOSTR	-.23	.09	-.76	-.01	.52
11	NSRG1	-.14	.17	-.69	.01	.53
12	ARLBU	.76	.86	.00	.13	.27
13	ARLXD	n.a.	n.a.	n.a.	n.a.	n.a.
14	ARLBT	.67	.81	-.10	.01	.32
15	ARLST	.28	.11	.74	-.03	.49
16	SH1LS	.34	.09	.75	-.06	.01
17	ALU1S	.29	.16	.65	.13	.53
18	ALT1S	.29	.11	.74	-.03	.53
19	SH2LS	-.27	-.05	-.67	.07	-.02
20	SH3LS	-.27	-.11	-.46	.00	.10
21	SH1LB	.80	.77	-.16	-.18	-.18
22	ALU1B	.77	.87	.00	.13	.28
23	ALT1B	.77	.88	-.03	-.00	.30
24	SH2LB	-.69	-.69	-.06	.19	.12
25	ALU2B	-.12	-.06	-.02	.92	.02
26	ALT2B	-.22	-.17	-.08	.47	.11
27	SH3LB	-.57	-.52	-.16	.15	.22
28	ALU3B	-.05	-.01	-.03	.47	.07
29	ALT3B	-.04	-.04	-.00	-.00	.01

n.a.—not applicable

Table 3-4
FACTOR LOADINGS FOR SIMULATED
BEER PURCHASING STATISTICS,
BASED ON ANALYSIS SAMPLE:
ACTUAL NUMBER OF TRIPS TIMES THREE

Variable		Principal	Varimax rotated factors			
No.	Name	Component	1	2	3	4
1	BRAND	-.70	-.64	-.08	.05	.42
2	UNPTP	.23	.31	.08	.67	-.03
3	UNITS	-.00	.24	.18	.36	.64
4	UNIDE	n.a.	n.a.	n.a.	n.a.	n.a.
5	TRIPS	-.11	.23	.04	-.05	.85
6	STORE	-.55	-.07	-.77	.07	.24
7	NOBRR	-.69	-.49	.02	.06	.83
8	NBRXD	n.a.	n.a.	n.a.	n.a.	n.a.
9	NBRG1	-.62	-.42	.03	.06	.78
10	NOSTR	-.44	.14	-.62	-.02	.64
11	NSRG1	-.41	.16	-.58	-.04	.64
12	ARLBU	.64	.82	.11	.14	.09
13	ARLXD	n.a.	n.a.	n.a.	n.a.	n.a.
14	ARLBT	.44	.68	-.00	-.01	.18
15	ARLST	.45	.10	.82	.04	.10
16	SH1LS	.53	.09	.84	-.21	-.03
17	ALU1S	.44	.22	.75	.19	.24
18	ALT1S	.45	.10	.84	.03	.12
19	SH2LS	-.49	-.09	-.78	.16	.02
20	SH3LS	-.35	-.08	-.50	.16	.04
21	SH1LB	.81	.82	.16	-.23	-.21
22	ALU1B	.65	.84	.11	.14	.10
23	ALT1B	.64	.80	.08	.02	.02
24	SH2LB	-.66	-.71	-.11	.27	.08
25	ALU2B	-.06	.02	-.02	.78	.00
26	ALT2B	-.22	-.18	-.05	.37	.04
27	SH3LB	-.55	-.56	-.07	.14	.16
28	ALU3B	-.13	-.01	-.08	.68	.04
29	ALT3B	-.19	-.10	-.12	.33	.05

n.a.—not applicable

The loadings obtained from a factor analysis of a simulation based on the coffee sample are presented in Table 3-5. This simulation utilized the same number of shopping trips as observed for each family in the actual coffee sample; therefore, it is of the SIM X 1 type. The loadings may be compared with those for the actual coffee data, which were represented in Table 2-6. The average number of trips for all families in the simulation (and in the actual sample) is 21.1, which is almost the same as for the beer SIM X 1. The standard deviation of the number of coffee trips is only half as large as that for beer, however, so the two simulations cannot be expected to yield identical results.

The pattern of loadings for the coffee simulation is almost the same as the one discussed previously for beer. Average run length is highly correlated with loyalty in both cases, although there is a tendency for run lengths in the first loyal store to be correlated with activity as well. The only real discrepancy between the two simulations occurs in connection with the statistics for number of runs. For coffee, these measures are loaded most highly on loyalty while the reverse is true for beer. The absolute discrepancies are not large, however, and the direction of the effect suggests that it is caused by the difference in the variance of activity for the two products. Since the standard deviation of the number of coffee trips is only half as large as that for beer, the tendency for the number of runs in a Bernoulli process to be correlated with total activity would not be expected to come through as strongly for the former product.

A comparison of the factor loadings for the coffee simulation with their counterparts for the actual coffee sample shows that the two sets of data produce similar factor patterns (except for the consistency factor). Most of the high loadings for the first four factors in Tables 2-6 and 3-5 are within a few percentage points of one another.

The strong correspondence between the factor structures for the simulated and the actual coffee has clear implications. Brand and store choice behavior for coffee approximates a zero order Markov process to a much greater extent than is the case for beer. In fact, there is no evidence that a simple zero order process is not sufficient to explain coffee-purchasing behavior satisfactorily. This finding is consistent with those of Frank (1960, 1962) and Massy (1966), which were also based on coffee-purchasing behavior. Morrison (1965 a, b) rejects the Bernoulli hypothesis (using a two-sided test), though he finds that coffee purchase probabilities are nearly zero order—especially for heavy users of the product.[4] The present findings indicate that whatever Markov properties may be exhibited by coffee purchasers do not affect the aggregative purchasing statistics. The opposite is true for beer, for which the aggregative statistics seem to show up departures from a zero order switching process.

Table 3-5
FACTOR LOADINGS FOR SIMULATED
COFFEE PURCHASING STATISTICS.
BASED ON ANALYSIS SAMPLE:
ACTUAL NUMBER OF TRIPS

Variable		Principal	Varimax rotated factors			
No.	Name	Component	1	2	3	4
1	BRAND	-.72	-.72	-.24	.01	.27
2	UNPTP	.37	.29	.11	.80	-.03
3	UNITS	.11	.12	-.07	.42	.80
4	UNIDE	n.a.	n.a.	n.a.	n.a.	n.a.
5	TRIPS	-.14	-.05	-.17	-.19	.91
6	STORE	-.60	-.16	-.83	-.07	-.04
7	NOBRR	-.76	-.73	-.29	-.00	.54
8	NBRXD	n.a.	n.a.	n.a.	n.a.	n.a.
9	NBRG1	-.67	-.67	-.24	.02	.52
10	NOSTR	-.64	-.16	-.91	-.02	.21
11	NSRG1	-.62	-.17	-.87	-.01	.22
12	ARLBU	.78	.87	.06	.24	.25
13	ARLXD	n.a.	n.a.	n.a.	n.a.	n.a.
14	ARLBT	.71	.83	.04	-.11	.31
15	ARLST	.45	.11	.63	-.13	.67
16	SH1LS	.61	.13	.89	.02	.06
17	ALU1S	.57	.25	.60	.32	.59
18	ALT1S	.44	.10	.63	-.15	.70
19	SH2LS	-.58	-.13	-.83	-.00	-.07
20	SH3LS	-.35	-.08	-.51	-.05	.03
21	SH1LB	.76	.80	.18	-.11	-.10
22	ALU1B	.80	.88	.08	.25	.27
23	ALT1B	.72	.85	.05	-.14	.33
24	SH2LB	-.64	-.70	-.13	.14	.04
25	ALU2B	.05	-.02	.05	.63	-.04
26	ALT2B	-.15	-.16	-.05	.16	.07
27	SH3LB	-.56	-.58	-.15	.08	.21
28	ALU3B	.02	-.03	.03	.41	.02
29	ALT3B	-.01	-.03	-.00	.24	-.00

n.a—not applicable

A SIM X 1 and a SIM X 3 were also performed for tea. The first produced factor loadings that are almost the same as those given by the actual data, as shown in Table 2-7. The factor pattern for the second simulation differed from the one for the smaller sample size in exactly the same way as observed earlier for the two beer simulations. Our major conclusion is based on the results of the SIM X 1; a zero order probability process is sufficient to account for the structure of the purchasing dimensions observed for tea.

RECONCILIATION OF RESULTS WITH THEORY.

The empirical results just presented provide insight into the effects of alternative probability processes for brand and store switching on the summary statistics often used for describing loyalty. These ideas can be followed up in a more formal manner through a mathematical analysis of some simple models involving zero- and first-order Markov processes.

Consider the following expressions for *expected run length* and *expected number of runs* for two-state zero- and first-order Markov processes. Define the following quantities:

π_1 and π_2 The elements of the stationary probability vector for a Markov process. For the zero-order process, these parameters are simply the probability of success and failure to purchase a given brand.

a_{ij} The elements of the transition probability matrix for the first-order Markov process.

N   The number of purchase decisions included in the sample of data for a given family.

Then:
Zero-order process for two brands or stores

$$E \text{ (run length)} = \frac{1}{2\pi_1\pi_2}$$

$$E \text{ (number of runs)} = 2N\pi_1\pi_2$$

First-order process for two brands or stores

$$E \text{ (run length)} = \frac{1}{2\pi_1\pi_2} \cdot \frac{1}{a_{12} + a_{21}}$$

$$E \text{ (number or runs)} = 2N\pi_1\pi_2 (a_{12} + a_{21})$$

Note that these statistics represent expected values for both purchase alternatives combined. The reader is referred to Wallis and Roberts (1956, p. 570) for an interpretation of the statistic for expected number of runs in a zero order process. It is equal by definition to: N/E(run length). Parzen (1962, p. 243 +) provides the basic theory necessary for the derivation of the formulas.

The similarity between the expressions for the two processes is obvious. Consider the *expected run length* statistic. A first-order process with small off-diagonal elements in its transition probability matrix will have a longer average run length than a zero order process with the same long run probabilities, and the opposite is true for a first-order process where switching is the rule rather than the exception. The *number of runs* decreases as the size of the off-diagonal elements of a first-order process decreases. The number of runs is proportional to the sample size for both types of switching processes.

Let us consider the effects of sample size on observed lengths of run and number of runs. Expected run length is independent of sample size for both zero and first-order switching processes, but it is intuitively clear that observed run lengths become constrained by sample size as N approaches expected run length. The size of this effect depends upon the type of process, as shown by the following numerical example. For π_1 and π_2 equal to .7 and .3, the expected run length for a zero order process is about 2.4. For a first order process with $a_{12} = a_{21} = .3$, however, expected run length is equal to 4.0. Now, for N's of only four or five it is clear that the distribution of sample run lengths will be strongly assymetric about 4.0. In fact, we should expect that the mean observed run length for families with only four or five purchases would be appreciably less its expected value 4.0. The same argument holds for the zero order process, but the effect will be much smaller because the expected run length is only 2.5.

The assumption that the values of a_{12} and a_{21} are less than .5 implies that families are more likely to repeat the purchase of a brand than to switch — this is realistic for most products, although one can think of examples where "variety" rather than "loyalty" is a controlling factor. Therefore, we may expect higher correlations between observed average run length and total activity for first-order processes than for zero-order ones, at least for most types of products. The correlations depend on data base constraints operating through the families with the smallest sample sizes. As the smallest sample size included in the analysis is increased, the correlations will tend to die away. We may also observe that the data constraint is likely to be more serious for first-order processes: analysts should be more restrictive in screening families with a small number of trips out of their sample if they are dealing with a first-order process than if they face a Bernoulli one.

The expected number of runs increases linearly with N for both the zero and first-order processes; so it is not surprising that number of runs tends to become correlated with total activity as the number of purchases in the sample is increased. The behavior of this variable in situations where the sample sizes for some of the families being studied are small is of some interest, however. This case is just the opposite of the one considered above for average run length. Since the expected number of runs for a first-order process with high repeat purchase probabilities is *small*, the observed statistic for number of runs will not be as sensitive to sample size variations as would be the case for an equivalent Bernoulli process. This explains why (i) number of runs is a better predictor of loyalty for beer than for coffee, (ii) the loadings on these variables tend to switch to activity in the simulation, and (iii) the correlations with activity increase as the simulated sample size is multiplied by a factor of three.

SUMMARY OF SWITCHING PROCESS ANALYSIS.

The relations of average run length and number of runs with sample size, given the type of switching process, is summed up in the following outline. These results have been observed empirically and are compatible with theoretical results for sample zero and first-order switching models.

1. Zero-order processes.
   a. Average run length is a good measure of loyalty. While it tends to be associated with total activity as well as loyalty when families with very few purchases are included in the sample, the effect is not serious.
   b. Number of runs is a poor measure of loyalty. It is correlated with both loyalty and activity when low activity families are present in the sample, but the relation with loyalty is swamped by the effect of activity as the range of activity by families in the sample is increased.
2. First-order Markov process.
   a. Average run length is good measure of loyalty, providing that families with very low activities rates are not included in the sample. If they are included, average run length becomes strongly correlated with activity.
   b. Number of runs is a better measure of loyalty than average run length if some families have very low activity.

The expected number of runs becomes more closely associated with activity for both processes as the range of activity included in the sample is increased, but the rate of increase is slower in the first-order process. The findings apply to both brand and store loyalty.

Comparisons of simulated and actual results show that the brand and store switching processes for coffee and tea are not distinguishable from simple Bernoulli models. That is, there is no evidence that the last purchase affects the probability of choice on the current purchase, as would be predicted by first-order Markov or learning models. The same is true for store choice behavior with respect to beer. On the other hand, the evidence clearly indicates that brand purchase sequences for beer cannot be adequately explained by a zero-order process. A first- or higher-order Markov model seems to be required for this product category.

LOYALTY PRONENESS

Are families who are loyal to particular brands of coffee likely to be equally loyal to brands of tea or beer? Do families who bunch their purchases of one product in a particular store exhibit the same type of behavior for other products? The answers to these questions depend upon the validity of the hypothesis of loyalty proneness, which is investigated in this section.

Cunningham (1956, 1961) was the first to try to determine whether the existence of brand and store loyalty tended to carry over across product classes. His answer was that there is very little generalization of brand loyalty; families who are highly loyal to one product show little more tendency to be loyal to other products than would be expected by chance. Store loyalty was somewhat more consistent across products, but the effect was not large considering the fact that many frequently purchased products are bought in the same store on the same shopping trip.

The existence of loyalty proneness is important in the present study because the loyalty patterns of families should be more predictable on the basis of psychological and socio-economic characteristics if they are consistent across product classes. Conversely, if a family is highly loyal with respect to one product but not with respect to another, our ability to predict the degree of loyalty for either is not likely to be very good. Finally, if brand or store loyalty is highly correlated for two similar products, as would be expected in the case of coffee and tea, for example, we should expect that the same predictors will turn out to be important in both cases. If loyalty for one product is largely independent of that for another, on the other hand, the set of explanatory variables which are able to predict loyalty in the two cases may well be different.

The analysis sample data were used to generate correlations between the loyalty variables for coffee and tea, and coffee and beer. The results are presented in Table 3-6. Only those families that purchased both products more than five times each are included in the calculations.

There is a consistent tendency for both brand and store loyalty to be positively correlated for coffee and tea. The coefficients for numbers of brands, share of first loyal brand, number of stores, share of first loyal store, principal component loyalty, varimax brand loyalty, and varimax store loyalty are all significant at the .01 level or beyond for drinkers of both coffee and tea. Only one of the activity variables, number of trips, is significant. The varimax consistency score is not significant, even at the .05 level.

The correlations for the eight raw purchasing variables on coffee and beer were obtained in a similar fashion and are presented in the second column of Table 3-6. The correlations are considerably lower than for coffee and tea, though the coefficients for number of brands and share of first loyal brand are just significant at the .01 level and the one for number of stores is significant at the .05 level. Once again, the correlations for the pairs of activity measures are not significant.

The hypothesis of loyalty proneness was studied further by finding the canonical correlations among the raw purchasing measures. The canonical correlation technique is best explained by reference to multiple regression. The important difference is that parameters on both sides of the "predicting equation" are estimated. Consider the following canonical correlation equation:

$$a_1 Y_1 \; + \; a_2 Y_2 \; + \; \ldots \; + \; a_p Y_p \; = \; b_1 X_1 \; + \; b_2 X_2 \; + \; \ldots \; + \; b_q X_q$$

The two sides of this equation represent linear combinations of the X's and Y's, which in the present case are the sets of purchasing variables for coffee and tea, respectively. The objective of the analysis is to find the two sets of weights (the a's and the b's) that yield the highest possible correlation between the two linear combinations of the purchasing variables. In the present case, $p = q = 8$, so a total of sixteen constants must be determined. On the other hand, if one of the two sides had contained only one variable ($p = 1$, for example), there are only eight constants to be estimated and the process becomes that of ordinary multiple regression with q explanatory variables. The correlation between the two sides of the canonical equation is the same as the multiple correlation between Y_1 and the set of X's.

If both sides of the canonical equation contain more than one variable, it is possible to construct more than one index of the sort indicated above. In this case, it is customary to call the pair of linear combinations of the variables that result in the highest canonical correlation the "first canonical variate" in the set. If a second index is desired, we must find the pair of linear combinations that results in the second highest correlation between the two sides of the equation *and* is uncorrelated with the first canonical variate. This is called the "second canonical variate." The third, fourth, and subsequent canonical variates

Table 3-6

CORRELATIONS BETWEEN PURCHASING VARIABLES
FOR COFFEE AND TEA, AND COFFEE AND BEER:
ANALYSIS SAMPLE

Variable	Coffee and Tea	Coffee and Beer
Number of brands	.31**	.24**
Share 1 loyal brand	.28**	.19**
Number of stores	.49**	.17**
Share 1 loyal store	.47**	.10
Total units	.04	.02
Units/trip	.10	.13
Units on deal	.08	n.a.
Total trips	.26**	.00
P.C. loyalty	.43**	
Brand loyalty varimax	.37**	
Store loyalty varimax	.49**	
Consistency varimax	.03	
Activity varimax	.01	
Sample size	260	179

 * Significant at the .05 level
** Significant at the .01 level
n.a. not applicable

may be determined in a similar manner, until the minimum of p and q is reached. The reader is referred to Cooley and Lohnes (1962, p. 35) for an introductory exposition of canonical correlation, or to T.W. Anderson (1958, p. 288) for an advanced treatment of the subject.

Canonical correlation of the raw purchasing variables for coffee and tea produced interesting results. The correlation between the two indices for the first canonical variate in the analysis sample is 0.58. That is, the best linear combination of the eight coffee variables accounts for some 34 percent of the variance of the best linear combination of the tea variables. The weights on each side of the equation are presented in Table 3-7. They have been standardized to eliminate differences due to the dimensionality of the various variables and can be interpreted in more or less the same manner as factor loadings (except that they are not constrained to the interval between -1 and +1)

The largest standardized weight in each column is for number of stores. The second largest for coffee is on share of the first loyal store, while number of brands is second in importance for tea. The weights for the other variables are all fairly small, so we are safe in concluding

Table 3-7

STANDARDIZED WEIGHTS FOR THE FIRST
CANONICAL VARIATE: RAW PURCHASING VARIABLES
FOR COFFEE AND TEA, ANALYSIS SAMPLE

Variable	Coffee	Tea
Number of brands	-.24	.43
Share of 1 loyal brand	-.28	.12
Number of stores	.58	.70
Share 1 loyal store	-.42	-.12
Total units	.27	.13
Units/trip	-.32	-.08
Units on deal	-.16	-.04
Total trips	-.23	-.08

Correlation	.58
Squared correlation	.35
Sample size	260

that the four variables just mentioned account for the bulk of the variance of the first canonical variate. The pattern suggests that the strongest dimension of purchasing behavior that is common to both coffee and tea is related to store loyalty. This interpretation is especially clear for coffee. For tea, it appears that families who purchase in a large number of stores also buy more than an average number of brands. This finding is consistent with the fact that the number of brands of tea offered in many stores is smaller than the number of coffee brands. Families who purchase tea in a large number of different stores will have the opportunity—and indeed may be forced—to select from a wider range of brands than would be the case for coffee store switchers, since the selection of coffee brands tends to be more homogeneous across stores than is the case for tea.

The correlation for the second canonical variate for coffee and tea is only .37; this means that only 14 percent of the variance of the second canonical variate is common for the two products. The vectors of weights could not be interpreted for the second canonical variate, so we conclude that it does not represent a meaningful dimension of loyalty proneness. The same is true of the third and higher order canonical variates. The canonical correlation between coffee and beer failed to uncover even one interpretable dimension of common behavior. The correlation for the first canonical variate in the analysis sample is only .41, and the vectors of weights do not make sense. Apparently there is no strong multivariable dimension of loyalty proneness for these two products.

SUMMARY AND CONCLUSIONS

This chapter has been devoted to a detailed examination of the characteristics of the purchasing behavior dimensions identified in Chapter 2. We have focused on four general points: (1) differences in purchasing behavior dimensions across the three product classes included in the study; (2) the reliability of our findings; (3) the relation of the dimensions of loyalty to the underlying structure of the process that generates brand and store switching, and the impact of sample size upon the structure of these dimensions given a particular switching model; and (4) the degree to which our loyalty and activity measures are correlated across product classes. The first two sections concentrate on the differences in the factor structures for coffee, tea, and beer, and the degree to which these results are dependent upon the particular sample chosen for analysis. The third section is primarily concerned with the behavior of the measures for length and numbers of runs in relation to the overall share measures of brand and store loyalty. The last section deals with the intercorrelations of the major loyalty and activity variables for coffee, tea, and beer.

Here are our major findings:

1. There are small but systematic differences in the structures of the factor dimensions for the three products. Of these, beer tends to fall in a class by itself, while tea and coffee exhibit similar patterns of factor loadings.

2. The observed differences in factor structure are not due to sampling errors or errors in the particular data base used in this study, either overall or with respect to any of the individual products. A factor analysis based on our validation sample data for beer produced a set of loadings that are nearly the same as the ones obtained from the analysis sample. A factor analysis of a one year sample of data on coffee purchases obtained from the Chicago *Tribune* consumer panel yielded results that are very similar to the ones based on the J.W. Walter Thompson panel, which have been reported here.

3a. Inclusion of measures for average run length and total number of runs in the set of variables used for defining loyalty is worthwhile. This is especially true if the number of purchases made by some members of the sample is small, or if the underlying brand or store switching process is believed to be of first or higher order. These two types of measures play quite different roles depending on the sample size (number of purchases) and the switching process, however, so care must be taken to sort out the effects of loyalty and activity for any given set of data.

3b. The pattern of purchasing behavior for coffee and tea can be satis-factorily approximated by a simple chance model using observed brand and store shares as parameters. This is not true for beer. Both brand and store switching for beer seem to follow a first or even higher Markov probability process.

4a. Loyalty proneness is a meaningful concept when applied to coffee and tea. This is particularly true with respect to store loyalty. While there is also a tendency for families' degrees of brand loyalty to be correlated for the two products, multivariate analysis shows that this tendency is swamped by that for store loyalty. That is, the evidence indicates that both store and brand loyalty proneness exist for coffee and tea, but that when the stronger store loyalty compo-nent is removed from the data little of the brand loyalty proneness component remains.

4b. There is little tendency for either brand or store loyalty proneness to emerge when comparing coffee and beer. While the simple correlations for the raw brand loyalty measures are significantly positive, they do not account for nearly as much of the variances of the combined sample as is the case for coffee and tea. Mul-tivariate analysis failed to yield any meaningful measure of loyalty proneness for these two products.

The findings given above extend and illuminate the results given in Chapter 2. While not directly related to the problem of predicting purchasing behavior from personal attribute data, they are interesting in their own right and will help to interpret some of the findings to be presented in the sequel.

NOTES

[1] The results reported in this section were presented at the 12th Annual Meeting of the American Statistical Association, Chicago, December 28-30, 1964. A condensed report is published in the proceedings of the meeting (Massy and Frank, 1964).

[2] In retrospect, it appears that in determining the Poisson mean, it would have been better to subtract a constant equal to the minimum container size of each product that is available to consumers, instead of the value 1.0. The value one is appropriate for coffee, and probably for beer as well, but a somewhat larger value should have been used for tea.

[3] The last factor is highly correlated with units per trip and average run length in units for the second and third loyal brands. Given that the switching behavior of the simu-lated families is known to be random, it is not surprising that what was previously defined as "consistency of choice with respect to infrequently purchased brands" should be replaced by some other effect. Other things being equal, families that habit-ually purchase in large quantities may be expected to have high average run lengths, as expressed in units. On the other hand, the actual data show that average run lengths in units and trips are highly correlated with one another, and that there is lit-tle tendency for the factor to be associated with units per trip. This supports the idea that brand switching behavior for beer cannot be satisfactorily represented by a zero order probability process.

[4] The standard tests for the order of a Markov process (see Anderson and Goodman, 1957) will not work in cases where different families in the panel have different transition probabilities. Morrison developed a different set of tests that are designed to take these differences into account.

IV

THE DESCRIPTION
OF PERSONALITY
AND SOCIO-ECONOMIC STATUS

This chapter presents the results of our attempts to develop a complete but economical set of measures for describing a family's socio-economic status and the personalities of husbands, wives, and husband-wife pairs. The available data consisted of raw Edwards Personal Preference Schedule scores for husbands and wives and some of the standard measures of socio-economic status and life cycle. Summary measures are developed through the use of factor and canonical analysis techniques — much as was done for the set of purchasing behavior variables discussed in Chapter 2. The summary measures are included in the battery of variates with which we attempt to predict the purchasing behavior dimensions, beginning in Chapter 5.

A word about the use of such summary variates in the subsequent regression analyses: With the exception of the husband-wife personality correlation Z-score (to be introduced presently), all the summary independent variables developed in this chapter are linear combinations of the members of the original variable set. Substitution of the new variates for the original ones in a linear regression aimed at predicting some aspect of purchasing behavior can only serve to reduce the explanatory power of the model, since the coefficients of the summarization procedure are substituted for the unrestricted flexibility of the least squares fit with respect to each of the original variables. Why then do we wish to find summary variables in the first place?

The first reason is that the introduction of auxiliary constraints on the least squares solution often serves to sharpen the interpretability of the results — providing that the constraints have meaning in the context of the model. This is particularly true when the original variables are subject to a high degree of collinearity. In this case any attempt to estimate the coefficients of the individual variables must founder on the rocks of large variances of estimate. The constraint serves to stabilize the regression plane and reduce the variances of estimate for the remaining coefficients. The process of summarizing sets of variables by linear combination, as utilized in this chapter, is one way of introducing auxiliary constraints. If the constraints are successful in increasing the precision of the estimates of meaningful parameters the summary variables will tend to be selected and retained in the stepwise regression process used in Chapter 5, in preference to the original variables.

A second reason for using linear combinations of variables becomes important if non-linear regressions are to be utilized. Then it is possible to make transformations on the combinations as a whole without dealing with the effects of the separate variables. This may be important if the theory that leads to such transformations is formulated in terms of a general constellation of effects, such as might be represented by a factor or canonical score, rather than in terms of the individual variates. This reason is less important than the first one in the present context, where little, if any, theory exists to guide us in the selection of variables and transformations.

The major part of this chapter will be devoted to a description of the personality variates and the development of summary measures based on them. Socio-economic and life cycle factors will be taken up in the last few pages. This division of emphasis is justified by the fact that much less is known about the personality variates than is the case for the social and demographic variables. Moreover, the former are likely to be much less familiar to the average reader in the field of marketing than are the latter.

THE DESCRIPTION OF PERSONALITY

Our personality data base consisted of scores on the fifteen scales of the Edwards Personal Preference Schedule (EPPS). The set of scores was available for the husband and the wife of each family in our sample. The following paragraphs present an overview of our work with these data. This is followed with a more detailed description of the EPPS and our various analyses.

First, the literature on the Edwards test was reviewed to assess its adequacy as a measure of personality; the results of this review are summarized below and presented fully in Appendix B. Next, a number of factor analyses were performed to determine whether a smaller number of factor scores could be used in place of the fifteen original scores on the test (they could not) and whether the factors were similar for men and women (they were). Finally, a good deal of effort was devoted to an attempt to find ways of economically describing the personality syndrome of husband-wife pairs. Several canonical analyses were performed to find the major sources of between-groups variance for husbands and wives — which turned out to be heterosexuality scores — and the stability of the results was tested. Another factor analysis was carried out on a matrix consisting of the original scores for husband and wife plus their sums and differences, to determine whether any factors existed which were described *only* by the combinatory measures. None did. No unique combinations emerged as a result of this work, but a general trend toward similarity between husband and wife was found. We therefore calculated profile similarity correlations between each husband and wife pair and found a low but very significant tendency for husbands and wives to have similar profiles.

The final set of personality measures (to be used in predicting buying behavior) included the 15 original EPPS scores on husband and wife, factor scores on the first four factors for husband and wife, scores on the first two canonical variates for husband and wife, and the Z transform of the similarity correlation coefficient.

THE EDWARDS PERSONAL PREFERENCE SCHEDULE.

Although we were faced with a *fait accompli* as far as selecting the test for this study was concerned — that decision was actually made by others for the J. Walter Thompson panel — we felt it was necessary to examine the accumulated literature on the Edwards test to assess its reliability and validity as a measure of personality. Although we cannot claim that the review was exhaustive, reasonable effort was made to cover all pertinent studies through 1963.

The test was developed by creating statements parallel in meaning to H.A. Murray's (1938) list of needs. Definitions of the fifteen needs used by Edwards are presented in Table 4-1. This procedure assumes that different needs vary in strength for different people, and that the total pattern of needs revealed by a particular person expresses his "personality." (Personality is typically defined as a "relatively enduring set of predispositions to respond in systematic ways to given classes of stimuli," although there are important variations from this.) The test requires the respondent to choose which statement in each of 210 pairs is more characteristic of him; it is thus a subjective self-report and cannot measure unconscious needs. The survey of the literature showed that the test is transparent to subjects, and that in spite of its forced-choice format it can be faked without perfect detection by its built-in consistency scale. It is also affected to some extent by variations in the social desirability of the statements. These disadvantages — its transparency, fakability, and its contamination with social desirability — are offset to a large extent by even greater technical problems with "projective" tests and other paper-and-pencil tests, and by its relatively nonthreatening character and ease of administration. If the decision on what test to use had to be made again today (1964) it would be difficult to find a better candidate, considering this and the evidence on reliability and validity presented below.

Table 4-1

DEFINITIONS OF SCALES USED IN THE EDWARDS TEST*

1. Achievement: To do one's best, to accomplish tasks of great significance, of requiring skill and effort, to do things better than others.
2. Deference: To get suggestions, follow instructions, do what is expected, accept leadership of others, conform to custom.
3. Order: To have work neat and organized, make plans before starting, keep files, to have things arranged to run smoothly.
4. Exhibition: To say witty things, tell amusing jokes and stories, talk about personal achievements, have others notice and comment on one.
5. Autonomy: To be able to come and go as desired, say what one thinks, be independent in making decisions, feel free to do what one wants.
6. Affiliation: To be loyal to friends, do things for friends, form new friendships, make many friends, to form strong attachments.
7. Intraception: To analyze one's motives and feelings, observe and understand others, analyze the behavior of others, predict their acts.
8. Succorance: To be helped by others, to seek encouragement, have others be kindly, to receive affection, have others feel sorry when sick.
9. Dominance: To be a leader, to argue for one's point of view, make group decisions, settle arguments, persuade and influence others.
10. Abasement: To feel guilty when wrong, accept blame, feel need for punishment, feel timid in presence of superiors, feel inferior.
11. Nurturance: To help friends in trouble, treat others with kindness, forgive others, do small favors, be generous, show affection.
12. Change: To do new and different things, to travel, meet new people, try new things, eat in new places, live in different places.
13. Endurance: To keep at a job until finished, work hard at a task, keep at a problem until solved, finish one job before starting others.
14. Heterosexuality: To go out with opposite sex, to be in love, to kiss, to discuss sex, to become sexually excited.
15. Aggression: To tell others what one thinks of them, to criticise others publicly, to make fun of others, to tell others off.

*These definitions are abridged from the longer ones of Edwards (1959).

Reliability was found to be good for this type of test in both split-half and repeated-measures determinations — certainly good enough for group predictions in research, although probably not good enough for individual counseling. Corrected split-half reliability coefficients range from .60 to .87, with a median of .79, and stability coefficients based on two administrations one week apart ranged from .74 to .88, with a median of .83, based on data from Edwards (1959).

Concurrent validity, judged by correlations between the EPPS scales and other tests containing measures of similar variables, was good for eleven of the fifteen scales, fair for three (deference, affiliation, and change) and poor for one (achievement, because of its failure to correlate with the TAT measure of need for achievement). Construct validity, measured by correlations of the scales with behavioral criteria, could not be assessed for four of the scales (exhibition, affiliation, intraception, and change) because not enough research has been carried out on them. Construct validity was judged fair for the deference and succorance sales, and results were mixed on the validity of the achievement scale — some investigators finding appropriate correlations and others not. The rest of the scales were judged to have good construct validity, having been shown to correlate fairly well with the behaviors implied by the needs.

Taken as a whole, the research reviewed certainly justifies the use of the EPPS as a valid measure of personality, as long as one is willing to settle for subjectively perceived rather than unconscious needs. From certain of the research studies it was estimated that the maximum multiple correlation between personality and behavior would be on the order of .60, with average multiple R's being somewhat lower.

Factor analytic studies of the EPPS have not shed much light on its underlying structure except to show that it does not apparently measure the "sicker" aspects of personality picked up by the Minnesota Multiphasic Personality Inventory, a test developed to discriminate between neurotics and normals. The relatively low intercorrelations among the EPPS scales indicate that factor analysis would be appropriate in interpreting the meaning of the scales, but probably not very useful in measurement or prediction, a finding which we tested with our own data as reported below. It is possible to say with a fair amount of confidence — based on this assessment of the literature — that if valid and real relationships exist between personality and buying behavior, we should be able to detect them using scores from this test as a measure of personality. The full report on the EPPS validity study is given in Appendix B.

FACTOR ANALYSES OF THE EPPS.

As noted above, not much is known about the underlying structure of the EPPS from the factor analyses in the literature. We employed factor analysis on the EPPS for two reasons: to achieve a better understanding of the nature of the variables themselves and of their underlying structure, and to find out whether the set of fifteen measures could be reduced to a smaller set of factor scores which could then be used as summary measures of personality for predicting buying behavior. We were successful in the first aim but only partly successful in the second; too little of the variation of the fifteen scores was accounted for by the factors to allow the factor scores to replace the original ones.

Edwards (1959) reports that there are considerable differences between patterns of scores for males and females, so two separate factor analyses were carried out on the 892 couples of the analysis sample: one for each sex. Essentially the same factors were obtained in both analyses. The data for men and women were standardized each on their own mean, combined into one sample of 1784 and factor-analyzed a third time; again the same factors emerged, so only the results of the third analysis will be reported here.

The method of principal components (see Harman, 1960) was used to factor-analyze the data. Initial communality estimates used were the highest-in-row correlations, and the program was allowed for four iterations to solve for the communalities, which did not converge in that time. The orthogonal solution was rotated using Kaiser's Varimax procedure, and factor scores for both orthogonal and varimax solutions were calculated according to Harman's multiple regression method. Fairly clear factor structures emerged from both the orthogonal and varimax solutions, which are presented in Table 4-2.

The iterated communality estimates presented in Table 4-2 indicate that most scales have relatively little variance in common with the others; the greatest is 56 percent for the nurturance scale, and the least is 9 percent for the intraception scale. The median communality estimate is .33, indicating that on the average only one-third of the variance in the scales can be predicted by the other scales. This immediately implies that factor scores (which are based on the common variance) cannot replace these fifteen original scores, since a good deal of specificity would thus be lost. In fact, since reliability estimates were available it was possible to calculate the specificity of each variable (reliability minus communality). These ranged from a low of .19 for affiliation to a high of .70 for intraception, with a median of .44, meaning that on the average roughly half of the non-error variance of the scales would not be reflected in the factor scores. Nevertheless, the factors may supplement the raw variates and it is possible that the communality thus defined will be related to purchasing behavior in its own right.

The first orthogonal (unrotated) factor seems to be a general factor, with high loadings on nine of the fifteen scales (for clarity of interpreta-

Table 4-2
ORTHOGONAL AND VARIMAX FACTOR ANALYSES OF THE EPPS

Variables	Principal component factors				Varimax rotated factors				Communalities
	1	2	3	4	1	2	3	4	
1. Achievement	-0.278	-0.288	-0.146	-0.113	-0.429	-0.058	0.057	-0.062	.197
2. Deference	0.445	-0.265	-0.141	-0.133	0.053	-0.385	-0.363	-0.155	.309
3. Order	0.308	-0.497	0.010	0.094	-0.018	-0.582	-0.045	-0.098	.353
4. Exhibition	-0.403	0.122	-0.096	-0.044	-0.263	0.310	0.123	0.091	.190
5. Autonomy	-0.277	-0.024	0.207	0.229	-0.031	0.037	0.400	0.100	.178
6. Affiliation	0.438	0.454	-0.334	-0.079	0.324	0.180	-0.587	0.183	.513
7. Intraception	0.159	-0.099	-0.193	-0.118	-0.073	-0.116	-0.257	-0.039	.088
8. Succorance	0.210	0.264	0.370	-0.078	0.439	0.136	0.058	-0.206	.259
9. Dominance	-0.454	0.008	-0.173	-0.377	-0.475	0.356	-0.020	-0.161	.375
10. Abasement	0.476	-0.009	0.266	0.064	0.459	-0.261	-0.058	-0.141	.304
11. Nurturance	0.612	0.422	0.092	-0.045	0.647	0.058	-0.372	-0.037	.559
12. Change	-0.217	0.276	-0.344	0.462	-0.064	0.172	0.034	0.649	.426
13. Endurance	0.219	-0.567	-0.087	0.139	-0.150	-0.611	-0.032	-0.020	.396
14. Heterosexual	-0.484	0.215	0.061	0.028	-0.171	0.399	0.294	0.103	.286
15. Aggression	-0.452	-0.074	0.333	-0.053	-0.176	0.177	0.476	-0.185	.328
Percent of Communality	33	20	11	8	31	30	25	14	72

tion a factor loading over .30 was considered "high," although anything over about .08 is significant). It is also bipolar in nature, with positive loadings on nurturance, abasement, deference, and affiliation and negative loadings on heterosexuality, dominance, aggression, and exhibition. Generally this seems to be a "tender vs. tough" distinction, reminding one of Horney's typal distinction between those whose predominant interpersonal response is moving *toward* others, and those who move *against* others. This factor accounts for 33 percent of the estimated communality, or about one-ninth of the total variance of the test scores.

The second orthogonal factor also has high loadings for affiliation and nurturance on the positive end, but the negative side is defined by endurance and order. No particular psychological interpretation seems obvious for either the second or third unrotated factors — none is to be expected, really — while the fourth seems to be defined solely by a high loading on the change scale. The intraception and achievement scales have no high loadings on these four factors; in the complete (15-factor) matrix intraception appears on the fifth factor and achievement on the seventh and eighth. Since the first unrotated factor seems clearly interpretable, factor scores for it were included in the final set of personality measures used as predictors of purchasing behavior.

The varimax rotation clarifies the factor structure a good deal. The first factor is more unipolar in the rotated solution, with positive loadings for nurturance, abasement, succorance and affiliation, and negative loadings for dominance and achievement. Instead of having a tender-tough bipolarity, this factor now is pushed toward the tender side, Horney's "moving-toward" kind of person. The second rotated factor seems to run along a dimension of orderliness-disorderliness, with heterosexuality, dominance, and exhibition on one side and endurance and order on the other. The third factor suggests the moving against-moving toward dichotomy rather strongly, with positive loadings on aggression and autonomy, and negative ones on affiliation, nurturance, and deference. The distinction here seems to be not tough-tender as in the first unrotated factor, but rather tough-weak. The fourth factor is again defined by one scale: change. Factor scores on the four rotated factors were also calculated for inclusion in the final personality battery.

DESCRIPTION OF HUSBAND-WIFE PERSONALITY SYNDROMES.

Since much purchasing behavior presumably reflects the tastes of both husband and wife, we searched for some way of combining the husbands' and wives' personality scores into a single set of family personality scores. Canonical correlation analysis was the first method we tried in this connection. This is a technique for identifying hypothetical variates which will account for a maximum of the variance between a set of independent and a set of dependent variables. In addition to the application discussed in Chapter 3, it has been used to identify what combinations in a set of predictor variables (such as a set of psychological tests) will account for a maximum of variance in a set of criterion variables (such as a set of job-performance measures). It combines the best predictors with the most predictable criteria. These hypothetical variates are called "canonical" variates, and have the property that the first canonical variate accounts for a maximum of the between-sets variance, the second canonical variate (which is linearly independent of the first) accounts for the next-greatest amount, and so on. In other words we used this as a technique for discovering the dimensions (or variates) that husbands and wives have in common. Presumably these dimensions can be used to describe family personality syndromes.

A number of canonical analyses were performed on different samples: the entire analysis sample (892 pairs), a sample of families whose purchase records were incomplete, and two random halves of the analysis sample, using standard scores derived separately for men and women. In all cases the first canonical variate is almost wholly defined by the heterosexuality scale, indicating that the largest amount of common personality variance between husbands and wives is accounted for by their heterosexuality needs. The Pearson r between husbands and wives on heterosexuality scores is 0.403, meaning that husbands and wives tend to be similar in their degree of heterosexuality needs.

The remaining canonical variates were not very stable from one sample to another, although at least five were statistically significant. This led us to perform the split-sample test on the stability of the canonical variates. The analysis sample was divided arbitrarily in half and the weights for the variates were calculated for one half and applied to the other half. If the weights are stable (i.e., not based on chance or error variance) the husbands' scores should predict those of the wives just as well in the second half of the sample as in the first, using weights derived from the first. The results of this test are presented in Table 4-3.

The relevant comparison is between columns 1 and 3 of the Table, which shows that shrinkage from one sample to the next was negligible for the first canonical variate but was considerable for the others. The proportion of variance accounted for by the second canonical variate, for instance, slips from .146 to .026. The only apparent reason for the slippage is the instability of the cross-correlations, (that is, the correlations between husbands and wives on the same variable). These changed in rank-order from sample to sample, and apparently the canonical procedure is very sensitive to this.

Because of the instability of the canonical variates beyond the first, only the first two were retained for the final personality battery.

Table 4-3
RESULTS OF STABILITY TEST
ON FIVE CANONICAL VARIATES

Variate	Lambda $(R)^2$	r (from test)	r^2 (from test)
I	.253	.456	.230
II	.146	.160	.026
III	.138	.136	.018
IV	.104	.136	.018
V	.086	.154	.024

(Actually, we should probably have retained only the first one, but we wanted to see what the second one might do by way of predicting purchasing behavior — in spite of its apparent instability.) The beta weights for the first two canonical variates, calculated using standardized scores for the entire analysis sample, are shown in Table 4-4. The values in this table are actually beta weights for the standardized values of the scales, so they cannot be compared across rows but only down columns. The first variate, as mentioned above, is defined almost entirely by heterosexuality scores. The second variate gives high weights to the same variables for men and women: positive on succorance, and negative on aggression and change. The second major source of covariation between husbands' and wives' personality scores is thus a combination of scores on succorance, aggression, and change, with heterosexuality creeping in to some extent. Canonical variate scores were calculated by multiplying these weights by the values of the standard scores for each variable, and are included in the final personality battery. Our canonical analysis showed then that the only stable combined measure of husband-and-wife personality was provided by heterosexuality scores. To check this finding further we calculated and analyzed two additional sets of measures.

The first of these was the set of sums and differences between husbands and wives on the fifteen personality scales. A factor analysis was performed on a data matrix which included the fifteen original scores for both husband and wife plus their sums and differences, for a total of sixty variables. The strategy here was that if any factors were defined solely by either sums or differences, we could assume this was a result of the combination which could not be accounted for by either husbands' or wives' scores alone; we would then have "family personality" factors. But no such factors appeared. All obtained factors could be accounted for largely by variations in husbands' or wives' scores alone. In fact, there was considerable similarity between these factors

Table 4-4
WEIGHTS FOR THE FIRST TWO CANONICAL
VARIATES: ANALYSIS SAMPLE

| | Canonical variate | | | |
| | Men | | Women | |
Variables	I	II	I	II
Achievement	-.169	-.029	-.077	.061
Deference	.205	-.362	.146	.240
Order	-.039	.060	-.044	.142
Exhibition	-.112	-.338	-.194	.062
Autonomy	.007	.136	.045	-.053
Affiliation	-.084	-.047	-.146	.071
Intraception	-.220	-.179	-.129	-.235
Succorance	.150	.527	.257	-.603
Dominance	-.215	.042	-.045	.058
Abasement	.032	-.147	.130	.029
Nurturance	.134	-.002	.082	-.018
Change	-.110	-.413	-.016	.466
Endurance	-.087	.083	-.020	-.061
Heterosexuality	-.699	.349	-.720	-.439
Aggression	-.106	-.500	-.146	.468

and those obtained by factoring the husbands and wives together in the same sample, as reported above. We concluded that sums or differences (or for that matter, averages) of the husbands' and wives' scores would add nothing to the predictive power of the personality variables. However, we tried one other way of combining scores before relinquishing this approach to the description of couples' personalities.

This involved calculating the *product* of the husbands' and wives' scores on each personality scale, and factor analyzing these products. The rationale for this was that the unique effects of combining personalities of husbands and wives might not be picked up merely by linear combinations (i.e., sums and differences), but that the interaction was rather a multiplicative one. Again, the factor analysis results were definitive: the varimax rotation of these factors yielded a factor matrix practically identical with the one for the combined sample described previously. Again we were forced to conclude that this combination of scores would not add to the predictive power of the personality predictor battery.

The results reported above suggest that the personality profiles of the members of husband-wife pairs tend to be generally similar. This implied that we should attempt to determine just *how* similar the profiles are for each family in the sample. To accomplish this end the correlations between the fifteen personality scores for the two mates were calculated for each family. (Each of these statistics is a Pearson *r* based on fifteen "observations.") The standardized personality scores were used in these calculations in order to avoid spurious effects due to differences among the means of the scores and to weight all the scores equally. The resulting correlations were subjected to Fisher's Z transformation so that their sampling distributions would be approximately normal. The Z-variates were included in the personality battery used to predict purchasing behavior.

THE DESCRIPTION OF SOCIO-ECONOMIC STATUS (SES)

The J. Walter Thompson panel provided information on eleven socio-economic and demographic variables that are of interest in this study. The information was collected from the families in our sample during the period between May 1956 and April 1957 so the data are comparable with the personality test results.

The means and standard deviations of the variables are presented in Table 4-5. The codes used to define the variables are appended to the table. The sample is somewhat older than the general population in the United States, but families of all ages are represented. The average husband and wife have both completed some college, although the sample also contains a great many families with only a high school education. The average family consists of 3.5 persons, has an income of about $5000 per year, and the husband's occupation is in the range of skilled craftsman to clerical or sales positions. Some 70 percent of the families in the sample own their home and more than 90 percent own a television receiver. Most own cars in the low price range and live in medium size cities.

It is obvious than many of the variables in Table 4-5 are highly correlated. This is particularly true for husbands' and wives' ages and education, but strong relations among the various economic variables may also be expected. Since high correlations between the explanatory variables in a predicting equation makes the identification of structural relations difficult or impossible, we felt that it was desirable to combine the eleven socio-economic variables into a smaller number of dimensions that can be used to economically describe SES. This was accomplished by the use of factor analysis.

Varimax rotated factor loadings and communalities are presented in Table 4-6. Six distinct factors were obtained.

1. *Life cycle*. The loadings indicate that older families have fewer members. This is consistent with the fact that children leave the nest and, finally, one of the spouses may die as the family unit ages.

2. *Education*. Husbands' and wives' education are highly correlated, as was expected. There is some correlation between this factor and income, but the relation is not a strong one. (Income and occupation become correlated with the factor for education as the number of factors extracted by the analysis is reduced, however.)

3. *Market Size*. Higher incomes and higher probabilities of television set ownership are positively associated with larger market sizes, as shown by the patterns of loadings on this factor.

4. *Income-Occupation*. Income and occupation are the only variables that are associated with this factor. Other correlates of economic and social class are taken care of by the other factors.

Table 4-5

MEANS, STANDARD DEVIATIONS, AND RANGES FOR
THE SOCIO-ECONOMIC VARIABLES: ANALYSIS SAMPLE

		Standard	Range	
	Average	Deviation	Max	Min
Husband's age	47.7	12.7	84.0	17.0
Wife's age	44.8	12.4	85.0	18.0
Husband's education	2.2	0.6	3.0	1.0
Wife's education	2.1	0.7	3.0	0.0
Number of persons in family	3.5	1.4	9.0	1.0
Income	50.5	18.8	76.0	9.0
Occupation	6.8	3.1	11.0	0.0
Home ownership	1.7	0.4	2.0	1.0
Television ownership	1.9	0.3	2.0	1.0
Car price class	1.4	0.7	3.0	0.0
Market size	19.5	15.7	40.0	1.0

N = 840

Notes:

i.   Ages of husband and wife are expressed in years.
ii. Education is coded as follows: (0) none; (1) 8 grades or less; (2) high school - 4 years or less; (3) at least some college.
iii. Income is measured in hundreds of dollars per year.
iv. Occupation is coded as follows: (0) retired, unemployed, disabled, other; (1) non-farm laborers; (2) farm laborers; (3) non-domestic service workers; (4) domestic service workers; (5) operatives, etc.; (6) craftsmen, foremen, etc.; (7) clerical, sales, etc.; (8) proprietors, managers, officials, etc.; (9) farmers and farm managers; (10) semi-professional; (11) professional.
v.   Home and television ownership are coded as (2) for ownership and (1) for non-ownership.
vi. Car price group: (0) no car; (1) low price car; (2) medium price car; (3) high price car. Data refer to the principal car as of the time of the enumeration.
vii. Market size codes are arranged in ascending order with increases in the size of the metropolitan area in which the subjects reside. The codes range between one and forty.

Table 4-6

FACTOR LOADINGS AND COMMUNALITIES FOR ELEVEN
SOCIO-ECONOMIC VARIABLES: ANALYSIS SAMPLE

Variable	Factor*						Communality
	1	2	3	4	5	6	
Husband's age	.909	-.134	-.105	-.079	-.280	.133	.96
Wife's age	.886	-.132	-.102	-.064	-.281	.030	.90
Husband's education	-.079	.672	-.083	.084	-.038	-.106	.49
Wife's education	-.142	.628	.123	.210	.089	-.067	.49
Number of persons in family	-.619	.062	.019	.073	-.145	.085	.42
Income	-.098	.248	.410	.416	-.248	-.391	.63
Occupation	-.098	.184	-.027	.630	-.032	-.006	.44
Home ownership	.108	-.019	-.054	.040	-.480	-.086	.26
Television ownership	-.110	-.029	.312	-.032	-.032	-.276	.19
Car price class	.032	.096	.067	.024	-.057	-.405	.18
Market size	-.035	.008	.652	.005	.112	-.062	.44
Factor variance	2.07	.99	.74	.50	.64	.45	

*The factors were obtained by the principal axis method and rotated according to Kaiser's normal orthogonal
varimax criterion. Sample size is 840.

5. *Home Ownership*. Families who own their own home, have slightly higher than average income, and are slightly older than average are negatively associated with this factor.

6. *Car Price Class*. Families who own expensive cars and those with low income and no car are at the poles of this factorial dimension.

The results of the factor analysis are reasonable in terms of both common sense and generally accepted theories of social class.

The communalities show that the factor analysis has been able to account for most of the variance of the two age variables, and a substantial amount of it for income. On the other hand, only about half the variation in education, occupation, and market size has been captured by the analysis, and the proportion is substantially less than half for the other variables. Therefore, we would not feel safe in using the factor scores as our only socio-economic predictors of purchasing behavior. Since it is likely that both the specific and common parts of the variables are important, it was necessary to reach a compromise with respect to the choice of socio-economic variables. Therefore, five of the factor scores and nine of the raw variables were included in the initial stepwise regression runs for searching out relations between socio-economic and personality variates and purchasing behavior (see Chapter 5). The two age variables were left out of this set because of their high correlations with the life cycle factor, and the car price class factor was deleted because it added little to the interpretation of the raw variables.

SUMMARY OF PREDICTOR SPECIFICATIONS

The results reported in this chapter led us to specify the following set of forty-five personality and fourteen socio-economic and demographic variables for use as predictors of purchasing behavior.

Various subsets and transformations of these fifty-nine potential explanatory variables are tested against purchase behavior data for coffee, tea, and beer in the next chapter. Work on the analysis sample data yielded a final regression model which includes twenty-nine predictors from the above list. This model was applied to fresh data from the validation sample with the results reported in Chapter 6.

Table 4-7

EXPLANATORY VARIABLE SET USED IN ANALYSIS
SAMPLE REGRESSIONS

Personality

1. The fifteen standardized EPPS scores for husband and   30 variables
   wife. (See Table 4-1 for definitions.) Standardization is
   based on the means and standard deviations for each sex
   separately.

2. The following principal component and varimax rotated   10 variables
   factor scores, for both husband and wife.

   a. Tenderness-toughness (principal component factor).
   b. Tenderness alone (first rotated factor).
   c. Orderliness-disorderliness (second rotated factor).
   d. Toughness-weakness (third rotated factor).
   e. Change alone (fourth rotated factor).

3. The following canonical variate scores for both husband   4 variables
   and wife.

   a. Heterosexuality.
   b. Succorance, aggression, and change.

4. The similarity Z-score for comparing husbands' and wives   1 variable
   personality profiles.

   Total for personality   45 variables

Socio-economic and demographic status (SES)

5. The nine raw socio-economic variates plus the family size   9 variables
   measure provided by the panel. (All the variables in
   Tables 4-5 and 4-6 with the exception of husband's and
   wife's age.)

6. The following five varimax rotated factor scores.   5 variables

   a. Life cycle.
   b. Education.
   c. Market size (size of city).
   d. Income-occupation.
   e. Home ownership.

   Total for SES   14 variables

   Grand total for predictor
   variables.   59 variables

V

EXPERIMENTS
ON THE
ANALYSIS SAMPLE

Our research strategy for investigating the relations between purchasing behavior, personality, and socio-economic status was to divide the data base into analysis and validation samples so that alternative models could be tried out without the risk of contaminating our final statistical tests. More detailed rationales for this approach are discussed in Chapter I. This chapter reports the main experiments performed on the analysis sample. The outcomes of these experiments permitted us to formulate a model which could be applied to the validation sample. Final results for the validation sample are reported in Chapter 6.

Our efforts at variable definition, reported in the last three chapters, yielded a list of some forty-five personality variables, fourteen socio-economic variables, and fourteen purchasing behavior variables. (Four additional dependent variables were added to the analysis at the time of the validation sample runs.) Not all of the explanatory variables could be used at once because of problems of collinearity or compatibility of interpretations. On the other hand, a wide variety of transformations of the variables in any regression equation was available (e.g., log transforms, inclusions of interaction terms, etc.). Yet there was little available in the way of either theory or previous empirical evidence that could help in making the necessary choices. Therefore we were thrust back upon our own data: the whole strategy of using an analysis sample was designed to allow indiscriminate searching for the variable combinations and transformations that provided the best fit and interpretations without running the risk of contaminating our final results.

Our work on the analysis sample is divided into three stages, each of which is described briefly below and treated in a separate section of this chapter. (1) Preliminary searching for variable combinations and transformations that provided the best fit to the data on regular coffee. This work was accomplished by using a stepwise multiple regression program for searching over the many combinations of variables that were judged to be potentially important. (2) Testing of the stepwise regression results on coffee with standard fixed variable regression runs, extending the experiments to include the other two product categories, and making appropriate modifications in the models. (3) Investigation of brand and store specific effects to determine whether the analysis should be enlarged to include these dimensions of purchasing behavior.

The first phase of experimentation was confined to data on regular coffee purchases because that was the data base for which the largest sample size was available and the highest purchase rate exhibited. This meant that there were a large number of families in the analysis sample for coffee, and that the purchasing statistics for each family were based on a larger number of shopping records than was true for the other product classes. Furthermore, the authors had previous experience in working with panel data for regular coffee (Frank, 1962, and Frank and Massy, 1963), which could be expected to be useful in the interpretation of the present findings. The results of these experiments were applied to the tea and beer data in phase two of our work on the analysis sample.

The third stage of analysis was instituted in order to check the possibility that personality and socio-economic status are related to the purchase of specific brands or the patronage of certain classes of stores. The main focus of this book is on the prediction of purchasing variables obtained by aggregating the data over all the brand-store combinations included in the panel. On the other hand, it is possible that certain personality types might be attracted to particular brands or stores, perhaps because of image configurations, even in the absence of any general personality-loyalty relation. Our work on this question is reported in its entirety in the third section of this chapter. Since data constraints limited the number of brands and stores that could be tested and the results of the available runs appeared to be singularly unpromising, this part of our analysis was not extended to the validation sample and hence is not treated in Chapter 6.

STEPWISE MULTIPLE REGRESSION:
REGULAR COFFEE DATA

Three experiments were tried using stepwise multiple regression based on regular coffee purchasing behavior. Each experiment was aimed at sharpening our formulation of the personality and socio-economic variables.

TESTS ON SUBSETS OF EXPLANATORY VARIABLES.

The first experiment consisted of running nine stepwise multiple regressions, each of which was based on the initial set of forty-five personality and fourteen socio-economic variables. Each of the nine regressions was aimed at predicting a different dimension of regular coffee purchasing behavior, namely:
1. Overall loyalty principal component factor score.
2. Activity varimax factor score.
3. Brand loyalty varimax factor score.
4. Store loyalty varimax factor score.
5. Consistency varimax factor score.
6. Proportion spent on first loyal brand.
7. Proportion spent on first loyal store.
8. Pounds per trip.
9. Proportion of pounds purchased on a deal.

The coffee data base provided a substantially larger sample size, 629 households, than did that for either tea (376) or beer (237). The first five dependent variables are the summary measures generated by the factor analyses described in Chapter 2. The next two are the raw purchase variables which received a major weight in determining a household's brand and store varimax loyalty scores, respectively. They were included as an internal check on the results associated with the varimax scores. The last two dependent variables are dimensions of purchasing behavior which did not fall neatly into one of the factors for which scores were generated.

In this and the two experiments which followed, we make use of a stepwise multiple regression program developed by the Health Sciences Computing Facility at the University of California, Los Angeles (Dixon, 1964). The program is basically a least squares searching mechanism. It starts by computing the F ratio (the square of the more familiar t-ratio) that would be associated with each variable if it were the only one included in the equation aimed at predicting a given dependent variable. It chooses the variable for inclusion in the equation that has the highest F ratio, providing that the ratio is larger than the one set by the user as the minimum F required for inclusion. After it has made this first choice it computes the F ratio for each of the remaining fifty-eight variables assuming that the new variable will be added to the equation which already contains the first variable. Once more the variable chosen for addition is the one associated with the highest F, provided that it is over the minimum specified by the user. Each time a new variable is added the F ratios for each of the variables in the equation are tested to see if they have fallen under the F level required for deletion. If they have, they are deleted. The program keeps on cycling — adding variables and checking for deletion — until it reaches a point where no variable passes the F ratio for inclusion and those which have remained in the equation are in excess of the F ratio specified for deletion. The program can be thought of as searching the least squares gradient looking for the best set of predictors, subject to the constraints on statistical significance set by the user.

In our analyses the F-ratio for inclusion was .250 and that for deletion was .120. These are relatively lenient tests. We preferred to take a greater risk of including something that was irrelevant at this stage, as opposed to excluding a variable that might later turn out to be of importance.

The principal objective of this first experiment was to provide a basis for choosing which measure of personality (standard Z, varimax-principal component or canonical scores) should be included in the final model. *The burden of proof for inclusion falls primarily upon the Z, varimax-principal component, and canonical scores as they are more difficult to interpret and/or involve more complicated assumptions as to the way in which personality characteristics influence buyer behavior than do the standard personality scores.* For example, the standard scores do not take into account the way in which the husband's personality characteristics are related to those of the wife (i.e., the personality structure of the household). Nor do they characterize the extent to which the scores for either the husband or the wife are intercorrelated. The Z and the canonical measures represent attempts to characterize household structure, while the varimax-principal component scores take into account the intercorrelations of the personality scores for the husband and wife, respectively.

Given that we have no theory for indicating how household personality structure or the intercorrelations should influence any particular dimension of buying behavior, the best we can do is observe the extent to which the searching mechanism built into the stepwise procedure picks out the alternative personality characterizations.

Our conclusions are based primarily on two summary measures describing the end result of the stepwise regression process: (1) the proportion of times that each of the four types of personality characterizations appear in the stepwise equations; and (2) the proportion of F-ratios for each type that are significant at the 95 percent level of confidence. The results are presented in Table 5-1. The measure "number of

Table 5-1
THE PROPORTION OF CASES INCLUDED IN THE REGRESSION, AND CASES WITH SIGNIFICANT F-RATIOS, BY TYPE OF PERSONALITY CHARACTERIZATION FOR THE FIRST STEPWISE EXPERIMENT

		Proportion of cases:	
	Number of possibilities	Included	With significant F-ratio
Standard scores	270	47%	10%
Varimax-principal component scores	90	21%	3%
Canonical scores	36	31%	3%
Z score	9	33%	0%

possibilities" is obtained by multiplying the number of individual variables included in a given variable classification by the total number of stepwise equations (for example, there are thirty standard personality scores which when distributed over the nine equations yields 270 separate possibilities for inclusion). The proportion of inclusions is the ratio of the actual number of inclusions to the number of possibilities. Finally, the proportion of significant F-ratios is obtained by dividing the number of cases where variables in the set are in the equation with F ratios greater than 3.84 by the total number of possibilities.

Both the proportions of inclusions and significant F ratios are greater for the standard personality scores than for any of the other three characterizations of personality, and by a wide margin. Since the factor and canonical scores could not be included in a regression that contained the raw personality scores because of collinearity problems, we tentatively decided to drop the former. The Z score was never significant in any of the stepwise runs and produced coefficients with signs and magnitudes that could not be interpreted, so it was also considered for deletion pending the results of the other stepwise experiments.

TESTS FOR HUSBAND-WIFE PERSONALITY INTERACTIONS.

We suspected that the effect of any one personality dimension, for example the degree of need for change on the part of the wife, might depend on the similarity of the husband's and wife's personalities as measured by the Z-score. For example, among households where the husband and wife have relatively similar personalities those with a wife with a high change score might exhibit a lower degree of brand loyalty than those households comprised of wives with low change scores, whereas among households consisting of husbands and wives with dissimilar personalities, differences in the wife's need for change might have little effect on the degree of loyalty exhibited. In other words, we hypothesized that there might be an interaction between the extent to which the personalities of the husband and wife coincided and the effect of any need on the part of one member of the pair on buying behavior.

We tested this hypothesis by running three more stepwise regressions based on regular coffee purchases to predict the varimax factor scores for brand loyalty, store loyalty, and consistency. The explanatory variable set included the fourteen socio-economic scores together with all of the canonical and varimax-principal component personality scores. Based on the results of the first stepwise run twelve of the standard personality scores and the Z score were deleted. The primary reason for deletion was that their F-ratios were lower than the remaining eighteen personality characteristics. Eighteen new *interaction* terms were created by taking the cross products of the Z-score with the remaining eighteen personality scores. The eighteen personality dimensions were:

Husband	*Wife*
Deference	Deference
Exhibition	Order
Autonomy	Exhibition
Affiliation	Autonomy
Change	Affiliation
Endurance	Intraception
Aggression	Succorance
	Nurturance
	Change
	Endurance
	Heterosexuality

The eighteen interaction terms together with the original eighteen personality scores (36 variables in all) were included as explanatory variables in this experiment. In addition, three of the canonical variables (husband's heterosexuality and succorance and wife's succorance) were used, together with the Z-score, to create multiplicative interaction terms. The results are reported in Table 5-2.

As in the case of the first experiment the standard scores outperformed the other personality characterizations. Apparently the extent to which the personalities of the husband and wife tend to coincide has little impact on household buying behavior, at least for regular coffee, and probably for similar types of frequently purchased food products as well. The results of the first two experiments are consistent in that they both favor the use of the standard personality scores.

Table 5-2

THE PROPORTION OF CASES INCLUDED, AND CASES WITH A SIGNIFICANT F-RATIO, BY TYPE OF PERSONALITY CHARACTERIZATION FOR THE SECOND STEPWISE EXPERIMENT

	Number of possibilities	Proportion of cases:	
		Included	With significant F-ratios
Standard scores	54	69%	17%
Varimax-principal component scores	30	0%	0%
Canonical scores	12	33%	9%
Z-canonical interactions	9	11%	0%
Z-standard score interactions	54	33%	4%

TESTS FOR NONLINEARITIES.

The third and last stepwise experiment served to test for suspected nonlinearities in the relations of the socio-economic and personality variables with purchasing behavior. Given our hypotheses as to nonlinear structure, an appropriate transformation was made of the scores for each variable involved. The transformed variables were then substituted for the original variables. Three stepwise regressions were then run for regular coffee using brand loyalty, store loyalty, and the consistency varimax scores as the dependent variables. Our hypotheses, the transformations used, and the resulting impact on structure will be described in the following paragraphs.

1. The standard personality scores. Earlier work done by the Advertising Research Foundation (1964), using the same panel but based on data for toilet paper purchasing behavior, led them to the hypothesis that a given personality characteristic influences buying behavior only in extreme cases — that is, only where the need expressed is unusually high or low in intensity. This suggests that the relationship between a given personality trait and buying behavior might take the form of the inverted S-shaped curve pictured in Figure 5-1.

If this relationship approximates reality, then the following transformation will tend to linearize it:

$$X^*_{ij} = (X_{ij} - X_{i.})^3 \quad ,$$

where X_{ij} is the ith household's score for the jth personality variable, X_j is the mean for the jth personality variable across all households.

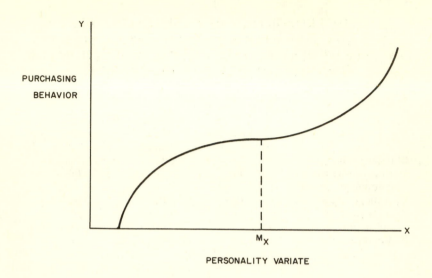

Figure 5-1. S-Transformation of Personality Variate

and X^*_{ij} is the transformed variable. The burden of proof falls on the transformed personality scores used in this experiment for the same reason that it fell on the Z, varimax-principle component, and canonical scores that were used in the first experiment: namely, because the transformed scores involve more complicated assumptions and are harder to interpret.

If the transformation is effective it should increase (1) the proportion of personality scores included in the final equation and (2) the proportion of F-ratios that are significant. The proportion of standard score variates included in the first (untransformed) experiment was .42 while the result for this experiment is .50. In contrast, the proportion of significant F-ratios was .16 in the first experiment compared to only .07 for the transformed data. Thus the pattern of evidence is inconsistent: the first result supports the use of the transformations while the opposite is true for the second criterion. Given the arguments about burden of proof discussed above, we interpreted the pattern of results as favoring the simpler formulation; namely the use of untransformed personality variates as in the first experiment.

2. The Z, Varimax-Principal Component, and Canonical Scores. Given that the standard untransformed personality scores are to be preferred over the transformed scores the decision problem that faced us changed from a comparison of the first and third experiments to a comparison of the results for the standard untransformed personality scores in the first experiment with the transformed versions of the Z, varimax-principal component and canonical scores in this experiment. Table 5-3 presents the relevant data.

Table 5-3

THE PROPORTION OF CASES INCLUDED,
AND CASES WITH SIGNIFICANT F-RATIOS,
FOR THE FIRST EXPERIMENT STANDARD
SCORES AND THE REMAINING PERSONALITY
CHARACTERIZATIONS IN THE THIRD EXPERIMENT

| | Number of possibilities | Proportion of cases: | |
		Included	With significant F-ratios
First experiment:			
standard scores	90	41%	12%
Varimax-principal			
component scores	30	53%	3%
Canonical scores	12	93%	8%
Third experiment:			
Z score	3	100%	0%

The proportion of cases included for all types of third experiment personality characterizations are somewhat higher than those for the first experiment. However, the opposite is true of the probability of generating a significant F-ratio. As in the case of the second experiment, this pattern of inconsistency led us to prefer the untransformed standard personality scores. One other piece of evidence supported our conclusion; namely a comparison of the R^2's and F-ratios associated with the two experiments (Table 5-4). The F-ratios for the third experiment are consistently less significant than those for the first experiment. The apparent increase in the R^2's for the three equations is primarily the result of an upward bias in predictive efficacy caused by increasing the number of variables included in the equation while holding the sample size constant.

Pending the results of trials on tea and beer, these results convinced us that standard, untransformed personality scores should be used as the basis for predicting the purchasing behavior variables in the validation sample.

3. The Socio-economic Status Variables (SES). Table 5-5 presents the F-ratios for each of the fourteen SES variables for the equations common to the first and third experiments. The third experiment contained transformations of nine SES variables whose titles are followed by an asterisk.

In seven of the nine cases (wife's education, income, occupation, home ownership, life cycle-varimax, education-varimax, and income-occupation varimax) we hypothesized that the underlying relationship between the variable and the store loyalty, brand loyalty and consist-

Table 5-4
COEFFICIENTS OF
DETERMINATION, F-RATIO, AND NUMBER
OR VARIABLES FOR EACH
STEPWISE REGRESSION EXPERIMENT

(Sample Size: 629 Households)

Dependent variable

First experiment	(1)	(2)	(3)	(4)	(5)	(6)	(7)	(8)	(9)
R^2	.12	.07	.10	.12	.09	.10	.10	.09	.09
F	3.60	2.33	3.78	3.70	2.74	3.13	2.46	2.13	2.44
No. of variables	24	23	20	24	24	23	28	28	25
Second experiment									
R^2			.12	.14	.09				
F			3.08	2.94	2.81				
No. of variables			27	35	22				
Third experiment									
R^2			.14	.13	.11				
F			2.81	3.05	2.29				
No. of variables			34	31	32				

(1) Over-all loyalty principle component score.
(2) Activity varimax factor score.
(3) Brand loyalty varimax factor score.
(4) Store loyalty varimax factor score.
(5) Consistency varimax factor score.
(6) % first loyal brand.
(7) % first loyal store.
(8) Pounds per trip.
(9) % purchased on deal.

ency purchasing dimensions would have the general functional form pictured in Figure 5-2. [1]

If our hypotheses were correct then the following transformation would result in a linearization of the relationship between Y and X^* :

$$X^*_{ij} = (X_{ij} - d)^2 ,$$

where X_{ij} is the ith household's score for the jth variable and d corrects for the origin of the process by taking on the value of the minimum X_{ij} in the sample.

In the case of family size we hypothesized that the underlying relationship would approximate that pictured in Figure 5-3.

The car ownership variable was coded in a particular fashion which led us to transform it by taking the raw variable to the .1 power. Non-owners of cars were given a code of zero, owners of low-price cars a code of one, etc. By taking the original value to the power of .1 we

Table 5-5

F-RATIOS FOR SOCIO-ECONOMIC STATUS VARIABLES INCLUDED IN THE FIRST AND THIRD EXPERIMENTS

	First experiment			Third experiment		
	Brand Loyalty	Store Loyalty	Consistency	Brand Loyalty	Store Loyalty	Consistency
Raw scores						
Wife's education*			0.38	.49		8.64
Family size*			4.44			4.69
Income*.		3.74			1.99	7.19
Occupation*			1.17	.40		
Home ownership*						
Television ownership			1.58			
Car ownership*			1.06	4.11	.38	
Market size	5.93	2.57		6.53	3.78	
Varimax factor scores						
Life cycle*	7.68	8.69	.84	17.22	9.81	28.32
Education*				3.34		
Market size	3.57					2.26
Home ownership			3.49			17.79
Income - occupation*	7.55	9.64		.36	10.26	
Car status	5.24	6.34			1.72	

*Variables subjected to transformation in the third experiment.

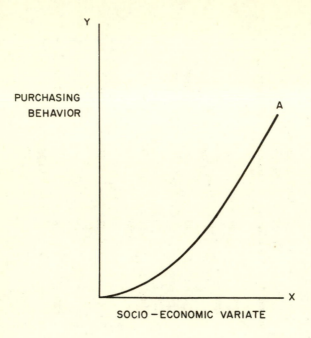

Figure 5-2. Quadratic Transformation of Socio-Economic Variate.

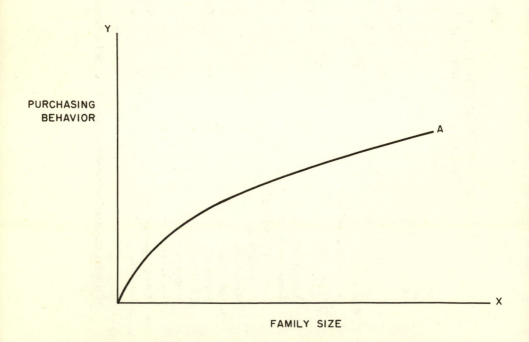

Figure 5-3. Square Root Transformation of Family Size Variable.

converted the codes into a dummy variable form (zero for non-owner-ship and one for ownership). Our hypothesis was that there would be a difference in buying behavior (e.g., store loyalty) between households that owned and those that did not own a car, whereas the price level of the car would be unrelated to household buying behavior.

On the basis of the contrast reported in Table 5-5 nine of the four-teen variables were tentatively eliminated from further consideration. Wife's education, TV ownership, and the market size varimax, as well as both the raw and varimax score for home ownership showed little promise of contributing to the prediction of purchasing behavior. The raw scores for both income and occupation were eliminated in prefer-ence to the untransformed version of the income-occupation varimax score. The raw score family size variable was dropped in favor of the transformed life cycle varimax variable. The car status varimax vari-able was dropped in favor of the transformed version of car ownership.

STANDARD MULTIPLE REGRESSION: ALL PRODUCTS

The purposes of phase two of our experimentation were to try out the independent variable set tentatively selected in phase one in a fixed variable regression model and extend this part of the analysis to include the analysis sample data for tea and beer. In addition, we tried out a number of minor transformations of the dependent variables during this phase of the study. In order to achieve these objectives we ran some forty 35-variable regressions (not stepwise) covering various dependent variable-product combinations. The results obtained from these regres-sions are summarized in the following paragraphs.

COLLINEARITY PROBLEMS.

Our first and most striking finding was that there is very high multi-collinearity among the personality traits for husbands, and also for wives. (Here we are referring to *within group* collinearity; the relation between husbands' and wives' personality scores was treated in connec-tion as part of the discussion of canonical variates in Chapter 4.) Sub-sequent investigation revealed what should have been obvious at the outset: The scoring procedure used in the EPPS is such that any of the personality variates can be perfectly predicted from the other fourteen. That is, the Edwards Test produces fifteen scales but has rank of only fourteen. One of the scales is redundant. The fact that the two groups are not *perfectly* collinear in our data must be attributed to errors in applying the test scoring procedures to the data from some of the re-spondents.

We have treated the general problem of handling collinearity in the Edwards Test elsewhere (see Massy, Lodahl, and Frank, 1966). For present purposes it was judged best to delete enough of the personality scales to reduce the collinearity to acceptable proportions. The choice as to which variates were to be eliminated involved a tradeoff between the contribution of each variable to the total collinearity of the set (see the reference given above) and its relative predictive power with respect to purchasing behavior. In addition, we felt that it was desirable to maintain symmetry between the variables included for the two sexes in order to avoid difficulties of interpretation. The variables finally chosen for elimination were achievement, dominance, and heterosexuality. Heterosexuality contributed the most to collinearity and was not strongly related to the dependent variables. Achievement and dominance were not related to purchasing behavior either, and the validity of the former scale is questionable as well (see Appendix A). The three scales were eliminated for both husbands and wives, thus reducing the number of explanatory variables by six. Elimination of these variables dropped the maximum coefficient of determination for the collinearity of one explanatory variable with all the others to a fairly respectable 0.45.

Additional analysis led us to drop the education-varimax variable and replace the life cycle-varimax variable with the raw scores for wife's age and family size. These two scores formed the major input for the life-cycle factor score, and they seemed to have separable relations with purchasing behavior. That is, they tend to have differential effects on such dependent variables and total activity and brand loyalty. Finally, the income-occupation varimax factor score was transformed in the same manner as had previously been used for life cycle. These changes were suggested when the model was applied to the tea and beer data. They left us with a final model containing twenty-nine explanatory variables: twelve each for husbands' and wives' personality, and five for socio-economic status.

DEPENDENT VARIABLE TRANSFORMATIONS.

The marginal distribution of several of the dependent variables (number of brands, pounds per trip, total pounds, number of trips, number of stores) resembles a Poisson distribution. On the other hand, the regression model assumes in part that the dependent variable is normally distributed. This assumption is particularly important for the validity of hypothesis tests. The following transformation was performed in order to bring the marginal distributions closer to normality:

$$Y_{ij}^{*} = \sqrt{Y_{ij} - 1} \quad ,$$

where Y_{ij} is the value of the jth dependent variable for the ith household.

Three of the dependent variables take the form of proportions. They are pounds on a deal, percentage of purchases made for the brand purchased most often, and percentage of purchases made in the store most often shopped. The regression model assumes that the conditional variance of the dependent variable given the independent variable is constant (homoscedastic). Suppose a positive relationship exists between some independent variable, say X, and one of the aforementioned proportions. Then some X's are associated with a higher expected value of the proportion than are others. The expected variance of a proportion is a function of its magnitude, and therefore, the assumption of homoscedasticity will be violated. The following arcsin transformation was performed to stabilize the variance:

$$Y_{ij}^* = \sin^{-1} \sqrt{Y_{ij}}$$

LOYALTY TO SPECIFIC BRANDS AND STORES: SOME EXPERIMENTS

Because of the importance associated with the study of specific loyalty to brands and stores we decided to conduct a more intensive set of experiments with respect to the prediction and structural analysis of these dimensions. Five experiments were performed. Three of them were concerned with loyalty to specific brands, while two concentrated on the prediction of store choice. All of them were based on regular coffee purchasing behavior.

A brief description of the nature and outcome of each one is presented in the following paragraphs.

BRAND LOYALTY TO PRIVATE VERSUS NATIONAL COFFEE BRANDS.

A two-way multiple discriminant analysis was run to determine the extent to which one can discriminate between households whose favorite brand was a chain store's private brand and those whose favorite was a non-private brand (i.e., a manufacturer's or a packer's brand). A household's favorite brand was defined as the brand that it purchased more often than any other. Only those households whose favorite store was one which carried private brands of regular coffee were included in the analysis.

The following twenty-two personality dimensions were included in the equation:

Husband	*Wife*
Exhibition	Achievement

HUSBAND	WIFE
Autonomy	Deference
Affiliation	Order
Succorance	Exhibition
Change	Autonomy
Endurance	Affiliation
Aggression	Interception
	Succorance
	Dominance
	Abasement
	Nurturance
	Change
	Endurance

Z-score

The following socio-economic characteristics were also included:
1. Market Size: not transformed.
2. Car Ownership: transformed by taking the raw score to the .1 power.
3. Life Cycle Varimax: transformed by taking the square of the difference between the original variable and the minimum score among all households.
4. Education Varimax: transformed in the same fashion as #3.
5. Income-Occupation Varimax: transformed in the same fashion as #3.

The discriminant analysis provides a multivariate test of the hypothesis that the means of all the variables are the same for the two groups.

The F-ratio for this test (with 27 and 194 degrees of freedom) was 1.0, whereas that for the .95 level of confidence is approximately 1.47. Thus we cannot come close to rejecting the hypothesis that the two groups of families could have been drawn from populations with the same underlying personality and socio-economic structure.

BRAND LOYALTY TO MAXWELL HOUSE COFFEE.

An experiment using multiple regression analysis was run in an attempt to predict the brand loyalty varimax stores for those households that purchased Maxwell House more often than any other brand. If there are differences in socio-economic and personality structure among brands one would expect that a brand-specific analysis such as this would be more likely to produce meaningful results than would an analysis using data on all brands combined. This brand and the one for which results are reported in the next section were chosen because they were the only ones for which data sufficient for separate analysis were available.

The variables included in this analysis were the same as those used in the discriminant analysis of private and national brand users except that the car ownership variable was omitted. The F-ratio for the significance of the whole regression is 1.05 (26 and 62 degrees of freedom) while the critical value at the 95 percent level is 1.70. The observed differences could easily be due to chance, given the available sample size. We are led to conclude that the use of loyalty data based on Maxwell House alone does not significantly improve the performance of the regressions. (For a comparison with the aggregative results, see Chapter 6.)

BRAND LOYALTY TO EIGHT O'CLOCK COFFEE.

The logic and variable specifications for this analysis were identical to that for Maxwell House. The F-ratio was 1.46, while $F_{(26,17)}$ is 2.19 at the .95 level. Once more there appears to be virtually no variation in brand loyalty associated with the socio-economic and personality characteristics.

STORE LOYALTY TO SAFEWAY.

Using the same set of variables upon which the Maxwell House and Eight O'Clock experiments were based, an attempt was made to predict the store loyalty varimax score for those families who shopped in Safeway more often than in any other store. The F-ratio was 2.76 while that for $F_{(26,11)}$ is 2.57 at the .95 level. The results are encouraging, but the specific personality and socio-economic variables that were most important in this equation are similar to those that were important in the prediction of the store loyalty varimax for all stores combined. In other words, there appears to be nothing that is structurally specific to Safeway.

STORE LOYALTY TO A & P.

The same experiment was performed for A & P with disappointing results. The F-ratio was .74 while that for $F_{(26,76)}$ is approximately 1.70 at the .95 level. There apparently is no payoff in segregating the data on A & P shoppers. The two store experiments provide little motivation for breaking out particular chain stores for individual analysis in the validation sample.

SUMMARY OF MODEL SPECIFICATIONS

The first two phases of our experimentation with the analysis sample led to the specification of variables and transformations that are used in the ensuing work on the validation sample. The final model consisted of the following twenty-nine variables.

Husbands' personality scores (not transformed)	Wives' personality scores (not transformed)
Deference	Deference
Order	Order
Exhibition	Exhibition
Autonomy	Autonomy
Affiliation	Affiliation
Intraception	Intraception
Succorance	Succorance
Abasement	Abasement
Nurturance	Nurturance
Change	Change
Endurance	Endurance
Aggression	Aggression

Wife's age: not transformed.

Family size: not transformed.

Car ownership: transformed by taking the raw score to the .1 power.

Market size: not transformed.

Income-occupation varimax factor score: transformed by taking the square of the difference between the original variable and the minimum score among all the households in the sample.

The pattern of results generated from the experiments based on specific brands and stores led us to drop this line of investigation. Therefore, the results for the validation sample reported in the following chapter involve brand and store loyalty without respect to the particular brands and stores involved.

NOTES

A positive association is presented for illustrative purposes. The validity of this and the other transformations which follow is not affected by whether the actual association is positive or negative.

VI

RELATIONSHIPS BETWEEN

PERSONALITY AND

PURCHASING BEHAVIOR

In this chapter we will present our findings on the relationships between personality and buying behavior. In accordance with our research strategy, the bulk of our results and interpretations will be based on data from the validation sample, since the data in this sample were in no way used in our efforts to develop a reliable set of personality and socio-economic predictors and a parsimonious set of measurements of purchasing behavior.

Before proceeding with the interpretation of these results, we will review our findings from earlier chapters on the reliability of the two sets of measures and on the concept of loyalty proneness. We will then examine the utility of personality measures in the understanding of purchasing behavior by assessing the amount by which the accuracy of our prediction of purchasing behavior increases when personality variables are added to socio-economic indicators as predictors. Although we will conclude that the percentage increase in predictive power which is added by personality variables is relatively small, many of the relationships between personality variables and buying behavior appear to be reasonably stable. Since the amount of variance in purchasing behavior explained by socio-economic data alone is also very small, the more reliable personality data are interpreted and some tentative explanations for the relationships are offered.

REVIEW OF FINDINGS ON RELIABILITY

From Table 2-10 we have seen that the reliability of the dimensions of purchasing behavior ranges from .46 to .93 with a median of .78. These results were obtained in a split-half reliability test, which means that, on the average, purchasing behavior on these dimensions measured in one six-month period predicts approximately 60 percent of the variance in the purchasing behavior in the following six-month period. Thus we can conclude that although purchasing behavior is not extremely stable over time, it is at least reliable enough to give rise to hopes that it can be predicted.

It has been held by some that consumer panel data are notoriously unreliable. It might be useful here to point out that data can be reliable over time without necessarily being valid indicators of the behavior that is being reported. For instance, if members of the panel found the task of recording and communicating their purchases an onerous one, they might tend at the end of the month to jot down an estimate of what they think they purchased; these estimates could be relatively stable from month to month (compared to the actual purchasing behavior), since they would probably be subject to the same kinds of memory distortion from month to month.

As noted in the appendix on the EPPS, the test has satisfactory reliability compared to other measures of personality. The split half reliability coefficients range from .60 to .87 with a median of .79. Therefore, the test is about as reliable as the purchasing behavior, which it is trying to predict. Again, this arouses hopes that the test can do an adequate job of predicting purchasing behavior, but cautions against optimism on the size of the relationships that can be expected.

A word about the concept of "loyalty proneness" also seems in order. In this study we are attempting to predict purchasing behavior for three beverages: coffee, tea, and beer. We are attempting to predict this purchasing behavior with personality data. The concept of personality is defined as "a relatively enduring set of tendencies to respond in given ways to given classes of stimuli." Therefore, we are testing whether behavior is a function of personality and not the other way around. In order to be a function of the "relatively enduring" personality variables, the behavior in question must also be reasonably consistent. We can therefore ask: "Can behavior in a given stimulus situation be predicted by the behavior in another, similar stimulus situation?" If purchasing behavior for coffee does not predict purchasing behavior for tea, very well, then we may be asking too much of our personality data when we require it to predict purchasing behavior for tea. From the data of Chapter III we saw that there is a significant relationship between purchasing behavior for coffee and tea, especially for brand and store behavior. But of the relationships tested, only eight out of thirteen were significant; the correlations ranged in size from .01 to .49 with a median value of .26; at most these are not very strong relationships. Purchasing behavior for coffee and beer is even less strongly related, with correlations ranging from .02 to .24 with a median value of .15. We can conclude that purchasing behavior for coffee, tea and beer do not predict each other very well, although there are unquestionably some significant relationships among them which indicate some consistency in this behavior. We must therefore not be too optimistic in our expectations for prediction of purchasing behavior from personality data.

One other set of considerations needs to be taken into account as we examine the relationships among personality, socio-economic variables, and behavior. As we worked to develop the best of predictors of the personality variables in the analysis sample, we discovered substantial relationships between the personality data and the socio-economic data and that there was substantial collinearity among the set of personality variables. In reducing the collinearity in the set of personality variables in order to render them usable in a multiple regression analysis, we removed those variables which were most highly correlated with the remainder of the set. These turned out on subsequent analysis to be personality variables which were most highly correlated with socio-economic characteristics. This is consistent with our strategy of asking, "How much variance does personality add to socio-economic data in the prediction of buying behavior?" But it also means that if we were using personality scores alone (with the socio-economic components left in) the total prediction for personality data would seem better than when we separate it in this way from the pure socio-economic variables.

In order to facilitate the reader's interpretation of the results, Table A-4 (Appendix A) presents an abbreviated dictionary of variables. Table A-4 can be folded out from the book to provide a quick reference for the tables that follow.

PREDICTIVE POWER

After our experiments with the analysis sample, the set of predictors was reduced to twenty-four personality variables and five measures of socio-economic status. For measures of purchasing behavior, there remained thirteen for the coffee sample, fourteen for the tea sample, and twelve in the beer sample. Using an ordinary multiple regression program, the twenty-nine predictors were regressed against each of the dependent variables. The results of this analysis are summarized in terms of predictive power in Tables 6-1, 6-2, and 6-3.

Turning first to Table 6-1, we note that in general the values of R^2 for the total predictive battery against the purchasing behavior variables are quite low (Columns 1, 5, and 9 of Table 6-1). While the

Table 6-1
PREDICTIVE POWER OF PERSONALITY AND SOCIO-ECONOMIC VARIABLES AGAINST PURCHASING BEHAVIOR: VALIDATION SAMPLE ONLY

	Coffee				Tea				Beer				#Sig.	#Sig.
	R^2 (1)	F (2)	R^2SES (3)	Fad (4)	R^2 (5)	r (6)	R^2SES (7)	Fad (8)	R^2 (9)	F (10)	R^2SES (11)	Fad (12)	F's (13)	Fad's (14)
1. ACTIV	.059	2.69*	.030*	1.61*	.068	2.18*	.038*	1.18	--	--	.034*	.80	2	1
2. ATIVT	--	--	--	--	--	--	--	--	--	--	--	--		
3. UNITS	.066	3.04*	.029*	2.30*	.072	2.31*	.041*	1.19	.074	1.25	.013	1.25	2	1
4. TRIPS	.047	2.10*	.023*	1.31	.055	1.74*	.017*	1.46	.074	1.25	.022*	1.07	2	0
5. UNPTP	.048	2.16*	.018*	1.64*	.043	1.34	.018*	.94	.101	1.76*	.012	1.87*	2	2
6. ATIVU	--	--	--	--	.075	2.42*	.035*	1.57*	--	--	--	--	1	1
7. LOYAL	.054	2.44*	.024*	1.62*	.056	1.78*	.025*	1.19	.083	1.41	.038*	.71	2	1
8. BRLOY	.050	2.42*	.024*	1.63*	.044	1.38	.014*	1.14	.083	1.43	.022	1.27	1	1
9. BRAND	.070	3.13*	.042*	1.39	.054	1.70*	.017*	1.40	.104	1.70*	.017*	1.40	3	0
10. SHILB	.045	2.05*	.026*	1.09	.047	1.46	.012	1.30	.093	1.61*	.026*	1.41	2	0
11. BCONS	.070	3.25*	.021*	3.02*	.028	.88	.007	.61	.079	1.34	.032*	.97	1	1
12. STLOY	.045	2.05*	.018*	1.47	.055	1.75*	.028*	1.05	.070	1.17	.018	1.04	2	0
13. STORE	.044	1.97*	.025*	1.04	.038	1.17	.021*	.63	.052	.87	.016	1.55*	1	1
14. SHILS	.034	1.50*	.012*	1.58*	.047	1.48*	.025*	.82	.058	.96	.015	.52	2	1
15. PUNID	.038	1.68*	.011*	1.45	.095	3.13*	.062*	1.30	--	--	--	--	2	0
Sample Size	1282				899				485					

*Significant at the .05 level

Table 6-2

NUMBER AND PERCENT OF SIGNIFICANT
(.05 LEVEL) PREDICTIONS,
BY TYPE OF PURCHASING BEHAVIOR

		Activity variables	Brand behavior variables	Store behavior variables	Total
1. Total battery	N	9	9	7	25
(SES + Personality)	%	69	60	64	64
2. SES only	N	11	12	8	31
	%	85	80	73	78
3. Variance added by	N	5	3	2	10
personality (Fad)	%	38	20	18	26
4. Number of significant predictions		25	24	17	66
5. Per cent significant		64	53	51	56

Table 6-3

NUMBER AND PERCENT OF SIGNIFICANT
(.05 LEVEL) PREDICTIONS, BY PRODUCT

		Coffee	Tea	Beer	Total
1. Total battery	N	13	9	3	25
(SES + Personality)	%	100	64	25	64
2. SES only	N	13	12	6	31
	%	100	86	50	78
3. Variance added by	N	7	1	2	10
personality (Fad)	%	54	7	17	26
4. Number of significant predictions		33	22	11	66
5. Per cent significant predictions		84	52	31	56
6. Sample size		1282	899	485	

values of F are all significant for the coffee sample, the predictor battery accounts for only 3 to 7 percent of the variance in purchasing behavior for coffee. The same conclusion is generally true for the tea and beer samples, although the sample sizes are smaller. While these significance levels are high enough (at least for coffee and tea) for us to be confident that there is some predictive power in the battery, the relationships are weaker than we had anticipated. Purchasing behavior is not well predicted by the best combinations of personality scores and traditional socio-economic indices.

Columns 4, 8 and 12 of Table 6-1 show the values of F (labeled Fad) obtained in a test to determine the significance of the variance *added* by the personality data to the overall prediction, given the amount of variance *already accounted for* by the socio-economic indicators. Results based on this test are noted in detail later.

Table 6-2 sheds some light on the patterns of prediction in Table 6-1 It shows the percentage of significant predictions for each of the three major groups of purchasing behavior variables: activity variables, brand behavior, and store behavior. Looking down the columns of Table 6-2, we note that activity variables are the best predicted by the battery, with 64 percent of the predictions on activity reaching significance at the 5 percent level or beyond. Brand and store behavior variables are about equally well predicted by the battery with 53 and 51 percent of the predictions reaching the 5 percent level, respectively. Looking across the rows of Table 6-2, we note that although 64 percent of the predictions for the total battery reached significance at the 5 percent level, 78 percent of the predictions using only socio-economic variables reached significance, and in only 26 percent of the cases did personality variables add a significant increment to the prediction that could have been made with socio-economic data alone. Personality variables also seem to add considerably more to the prediction of activity variables than they do for either brand or store behavior.

Table 6-3 gives a breakdown of predictive power by products. Looking down the columns of Table 6-3, we note that coffee is by far the best predicted of the three products with 84 percent of the predictions reaching significance at the 5 percent level, tea is second with 52 percent and beer is a poor third with 31 percent. The personality variables add a significant increment to the prediction from socio-economic data alone in 54 percent of the cases for coffee, but only in 7 and 17 percent of the cases for tea and beer, respectively. It is interesting to note also that socio-economic data drops less in predictive power for purchasing than either the total battery or the personality data alone. Beer purchasing behavior, however, is relatively poorly predicted by all of the measures in the battery. (Part of this is due to the lower power of the F test with smaller sample sizes.)

Let us summarize our conclusions on predictive power thus far. (1)

Purchasing behavior is relatively poorly predicted by the battery. (2) Socio-economic data alone has the best prediction record for purchasing behavior with 78 percent of the predictions reaching significance. (3) Personality scores add a significant increment to the prediction from socio-economic data in only 26 percent of the cases, and most of these are clustered on coffee on the product breakdown and on activity variables in the purchasing behavior breakdown.

One of the major questions we wanted to answer in this study was whether personality data add enough effective power for the understanding of purchasing behavior to justify the added expense and difficulty of collecting them. Given the results summarized above, it seems that we must tentatively conclude that they probably do not; but we must also note that socio-economic data *by themselves* do a thoroughly poor job of prediction on an absolute basis. Taken altogether, they are accounting for between one and four percent of the variance in purchasing behavior for coffee, and likewise for tea and beer. If this small a proportion of the variance in any set of behavioral data can be understood with socio-economic data, then it does seem worthwhile to try new predictors in an effort to understand the behavior more thoroughly, at least for research purposes.

PATTERNS OF RELATIONSHIPS AMONG PERSONALITY VARIABLES, SOCIO-ECONOMIC DATA, AND PURCHASING BEHAVIOR

Although the total predictive power of the battery is low, the percentage of significant predictions is substantially beyond the chance level. Thus it becomes necessary to examine those relationships which appear to be significant and stable, and to try to arrive at an understanding of their underlying nature. In presenting the results of this analysis we will consider all three product classes together (where appropriate). We will take up brand behavior, store behavior, and activity variables in that order.

We restricted ourselves in interpreting the results to those relationships for which the confidence level for the regression coefficient was significant beyond the .95 level. We considered other interpretive strategies in some detail, but deliberately adopted this relatively conservative approach. Other methods are clearly possible, and for this reason we have included the complete results of the regression analysis in Appendix A.

BRAND BEHAVIOR

Table 6-4 presents selected results on brand behavior. Five dependent variables were used in this analysis. We used two measures of loyalty, LOYAL and BRLOY, because they measure slightly different quantities and because using two such measures gives a better feeling for the stability of the results (even though the two measures are themselves correlated). In addition, we analyzed the relationship between the predictor variables and measures of consistency on second and third brands, the standard normal deviate for run length, and amount purchased on deals. The latter three variables have been oriented in Table 6-4 toward the high loyalty direction. That is, within each product class, above the dotted line, the determinants of "high loyalty" for each variable are presented first. Thus, the consistency score was left as it originally appeared; measure of run length (SND1B) was reversed so that a high value means long run length, and the dealing variable (PUNID) is presented with the signs on the independent variables reversed, since high dealing goes with low loyalty.

Looking first at the socio-economic variables, we note in Table 6-4 that high income and location in big markets generally means low loyalty. This is very clearly true for coffee and tea, and high income also means low loyalty for beer, although market size does not appear in the loyalty column for beer. These findings make a good deal of sense because people with high incomes and those in big markets, generally speaking, have a greater range of choice of brands than their opposite numbers. In the coffee data we also note that family size is associated with high consistency on second and third brands with low purchasing on deals. The latter is somewhat surprising since one might have assumed that big families, in order to economize, might purchase more goods on cents-off deals. For the tea and beer data we note that market size and income-occupation occasionally appear on the high loyalty side of the dotted line. For tea, market size and income are associated with high consistency on second and third brands, and market size is also associated with low dealing behavior. For beer, market size is associated with high consistency on second and third brands. Since the latter findings are rather unstable across products, we will be content merely to note them and will not hazard any kind of explanation.

Turning to the personality data and their relations to brand behavior, we must first note, as a caveat, that quite often husband and wife scores on the same personality variable relate differently to the dependent variables and therefore they have to be treated as separate entities. The most stable relationship between personality and brand choice behavior appears to be that between husband's endurance score and the loyalty variables. This comes through as a positive relationship in all three products classes and is perhaps the most stable finding in the whole set of relationships between personality and buying behavior. In the EPPS, the need for endurance is measured with items such as the following: "to keep at a job until it is finished; to complete any job undertaken; to work hard at a task; to keep at puzzle or problem until

Table 6-4
SELECTED RESULTS ON BRAND BEHAVIOR

(Variables listed are those for which regression
coefficients were significant beyond the .05 level.
Sign before variable indicates direction of relationship.)

	Loyalty		Consistency	Run Length	Amount purchased in deals
1. Coffee	LOYAL	BRLOY	BCONS	SNDIB	PUNID
	+HENDUR		+HINTRA		
	+WDEFER	+WDEFER	+HSUCCR	+HSUCCR	
	+WAUTON	+WAUTON	+WAUTON	+WDEFER	-WDEFER
	+WSUCCR	+WSUCCR	+WENDUR	+WENDUR	+WCHANG
			+FAMSIZ		-FAMSIZ
	-HDEFER	-HDEFER	-HAFFIL	-HAFFIL	+HDEFER
	-WCHANG			-HNURTR	+HAUTON
	-MKTSIZ	-MKTSIZ			+HAFFIL
	-INCOCC	-INCOCC			+WCHANG
2. Tea	LOYAL	BRLOY	BCONS	SNDIB	PUNID
	+HENDUR	+HENDUR	+HCHANG		
	+WORDER	+WORDER	+WORDER		-HDEFER
			+MKTSIZ		-MKTSIZ
			+INCOCC		
		-HORDER	-WEXHIB	-HDEFER	+HAFFIL
		-HCHANG	-WENDUR		
	-MKTSIZ	-MKTSIZ			
	-INCOCC			-INCOCC	
3. Beer	LOYAL	BLROY	BCONS	SNDIB	(No deals recorded in beer data)
	+HENDUR	+HENDUR		+WSUCCR	
	+WNURTR	+WNURTR	+WNURTR	+WCHANG	
			+MKTSIZ	+INCOCC	
			-HDEFER	-WORDER	
	-HORDER		-HORDER		
			-FAMSIZ		
	-INCOCC	-INCOCC	-INCOCC		

it is solved; to work at a single job before taking on others; to stay up late working in order to get a job done," etc. Taken together, these items seem to get at a need for completion and it makes a good deal of *post hoc* sense that this variable is related to brand loyalty. It is not altogether clear why it is the husband's endurance score and not the wife's which correlates so strongly with brand loyalty. It must be that the husband's preference for brands exerts a good deal of influence on the purchasing decision for these three products.

The other significant predictors for loyalty provide some interesting contrasts. For instance, in the coffee data, wife's deference score, wife's autonomy score, and wife's succorance score are all associated with high loyalty. Deference and succorance generally describe needs to be dependent on others, while autonomy clearly describes needs to be independent of others. Furthermore, while wife's deference score is associated with high loyalty, husband's deference score is associated with low loyalty for coffee. One explanation for this puzzling set of findings is that there may be two root sources of loyalty: one kind of brand loyalty may be based on strength and independence, or resistance to influence attempts of various kinds designed to get people to switch brand. The other kind of loyalty may be based on weakness and dependency. People high on the need for deference and succorance may be afraid to try something new or may get security and satisfaction from sticking with the tried and true. This interpretation is reinforced when we note that wife's autonomy score is associated with high consistency on second and third brands and wife's deference score is associated with long run lengths and with resistance to purchasing on deals. The latter definitely seems to suggest some kind of resistance to change based on insecurity or fear of the unknown.

To summarize the above idea, one can list the correlates for each factor in tabular form:

Factor A
Strength and independence
Wife's autonomy
Wife's endurance
Husband's endurance

Factor B
Weakness or fear of change
Wife's deference
Wife's succorance
Husband's succorance

This two-factor interpretation of the personality correlates of brand loyalty must remain a hypothesis, since new data would be necessary to establish it with any certainty.

Another interesting contrast is provided in the loyalty data for tea and beer. For both tea and beer husband's need for order is associated with low loyalty, and for tea, husband's need for change is also associated with low loyalty. It seems peculiar that both needs for order and change should be associated with low loyalty, although the relationship between change and low loyalty seems logically acceptable. The need for order measures, among other things, the need "to have things arranged so that they run smoothly without change." Why this should be associated with low brand loyalty for tea and beer currently defies explanation.

Again picking up the contrast in the way wife's and husband's deference scores relate to loyalty, we note that while wife's deference scores are associated with long runs and low dealing behavior, husband's deference score is associated with low loyalty and high dealing behavior. This begins to make some sense when we note also that in the coffee data (and to some extent in the tea data) the husband's affiliation scores are associated with low consistency, short run lengths, and high dealing behavior. Note also that husband's deference score is associated with high dealing behavior. It seems reasonable to assume that the brand switching process is likely to begin on the second or third brand rather than on the first, is enhanced by the availability of a deal, and affects run length. The pattern of husband's deference scores, husband's affiliation scores, and wife's change scores are all consistent with this picture; all but husband's affiliation score are also associated with low brand loyalty. One general interpretation of this pattern would be that husband's deference and affiliation scores measure susceptibility to influence attempts such as advertising and deals. We note that elements of this pattern exist for the tea data in that husband's affiliation and deference scores both appear on the low loyalty side. There is also a suggestion of it in the beer data; husband's deference score is associated with low consistency. On the other hand, for the tea data we must note that husband's deference is associated with low dealing behavior, which is not consistent with the pattern. In any case, this interpretation must remain only a suggestion since it was obtained from the data on the validation sample and longitudinal data on influence attempts were not available to us.

Among the other data of Table 6-4 two additional findings appear to be stable enough to deserve comment: wife's need for order is associated with high loyalty and high consistency in tea purchasing, and wife's need for nurturance is associated with high loyalty and high consistency in the beer purchasing data. Again, we have an interesting contrast in the tea data, since husband's need for order is associated with low loyalty for tea brands. We can accept the logical plausibility of the relationship between needs for order and high consistency and loyalty, but why husband's need for order should be associated with low loyalty remains inexplicable, although it appears both in the tea and beer data. Perhaps the husband in this case is seeking the perfect tea or the perfect beer and will remain restless in this choice of brands until he finds it.

Summarizing the findings on brand loyalty, we have noted:

1. High incomes and big markets generally mean low loyalty.

2. Husband's endurance score is associated with high loyalty for all three product classes. This is the most stable relationship between personality and the brand behavior.

3. Husband and wife's personality scores on the same personality dimension relate differently to the dependent variables, and therefore have to be treated as separate entities.

4. Brand loyalty may have two different psychological bases in the wife's personality scores: one based on independence (autonomy score), and one based on resistance and fear of change (deference and succorance scores).

5. Husband's preferences may play a strong role in brand behavior in families, considering the number and strengths of the relationships between husbands' personality scores and brand behavior.

6. Switching behavior may have a psychological basis in needs for affiliation and deference on the part of the husband, suggesting that husbands in high-switching families are more susceptible to influence attempts.

STORE BEHAVIOR

Table 6-5 presents the significant relationships between the predictors and the dependent variables measuring store behavior. Again, two measures of loyalty were used: LOYAL, which contains elements of both brand and store loyalty, and STLOY, which is a purer measure of store loyalty. We also used a measure of run length for stores, SND1S and we included proportions purchased on deals PUNID as another measure of store behavior. It should be noted here that two of the four dependent variables for store behavior are the same as we used in the analysis of brand behavior above. Again, the dependent variables are oriented toward the high loyalty dimension, relationships above the line indicating high loyalty and those below the line, low loyalty.

Turning first to the relationships between socio-economic data and store behavior, we note that again income-occupation and market size are generally associated with low store loyalty, family size is again asso-

Table 6–5
SELECTED RESULTS ON STORE BEHAVIOR

(Variables listed are those for which regression
coefficients were significant beyond the .05 level.
Sign before variable indicates direction of relationship.)

	Loyalty		Run Length	Amount purchased on deals
1. Coffee	LOYAL	STLOY	SNDIS	PUNID
		+HAUTON	+WENDUR	
	+HENDUR	+HENDUR		
	+WDEFER			-WDEFER
	+WAUTON		+FAMSIZ	-FAMSIZ
	+WSUCCR	+WSUCCR		
	-HDEFER		-HAGGRE	+HDEFER
	-WCHANG	-WCHANG		+HAUTON
	-MKTSIZ	-MKTSIZ	-WOMAGE	+HAFFIL
	-INCOCC	-INCOCC		
2. Tea	LOYAL	STLOY	SNDIS	PUNID
			+HNURTR	-HAFFIL
	+HENDUR	+HENDUR	+WORDER	
	+WORDER	-WORDER	+WEXHIB	
	-MKTSIZ	-MKTSIZ	-OWNCAR	+HDEFER
	-INCOCC	-INCOCC		+MKTSIZ
3. Beer	LOYAL	STLOY	SNDIS	(No deals in beer)
	+HENDUR			
	+WNURTR			
		-HINTRA	-HDEFER	
		-WAGGRE	-HEXHIB	
	-INCOCC	-INCOCC	-HABASE	

ciated with long run lengths for stores, and we note that interestingly, car ownership is associated with short run lengths for stores on purchasing behavior for tea.

The personality data again show a strong relationship between husband's need for endurance and store loyalty. This is clearly true for the coffee and tea data, in that both LOYAL and STLOY are related to husband's endurance. For the beer data, only LOYAL shows a relationship to husband's endurance score. Again, this appears to be the most stable finding across products in the store loyalty data. Wife's need for change is again associated with low store loyalty for coffee.

On store loyalty for tea, wife's need for order is significantly and positively related to LOYAL and to store run lengths; it is significantly and negatively related to STLOY. Put simply, this means that the woman with high needs for order is generally loyal to her brand of tea, tends to buy it in different stores, but has relatively long run lengths for particular stores. We might characterize her as a "long-cycle store switcher." Summarizing the results on store loyalty, then, we can say the following:

1. Market size and income, as in brand loyalty, are associated with low store loyalties.

2. Husband's endurance score is again strongly and consistently related to high store loyalty.

3. Husband's deference score and wife's change score are again associated with low store loyalty.

Some comments on the strategic implications of the brand and store findings may be in order here. If our two-factor interpretation of the nature of brand loyalty is correct, it would seem that the "strength" pattern, which includes high scores on husband's need for endurance, wife's need for autonomy and wife's need for endurance, is almost impenetrable combination. We might refer to these people as "unreachables." Once they are won over to a brand, it would seem very difficult to dislodge them. They tend to have high loyalty, high consistency, and to some extent fairly long run lengths. It is not clear where they stand on dealing behavior. The "resistance-fear pattern," which includes wife's need for deference and succorance, and husband's need for succorance may be somewhat easier to devise strategies for, but wife's deference is associated with low dealing behavior and with long run lengths; this highly brand-loyal person would probably need to be very sure about the qualities of the new brand before deciding to try it out.

The low loyalty pattern, on the other hand, seems to have somewhat clearer strategic implications. Low loyalty appears to be associated with high scores on wife's need for change, and with high husband's deference and affiliation scores. These are also associated with high propensities to purchase on deal, with short run lengths, and with low consistency on second and third brands. It would seem easier to switch this person, but it might be equally easy to switch him out of the new brand and into yet another. Most of the foregoing comments are based on the brand analysis for coffee, although elements of the low loyalty pattern also appear in the data for tea.

The highly store loyal family is one in which the husband has a high need for endurance. One strategic implication of this might be that, to maintain this kind of loyal clientele, the store should retain a relatively stable shelf and product organization, since this person has relatively high completion needs.

ACTIVITY VARIABLES

Table 6-6 presents the significant results on the activity variables. Within each product, variables associated with high activity appear above the dotted line; those associated with low activity appear below the dotted line.

Again turning to the socio-economic data we see that families who purchase a lot of coffee are big families, have a car, and live in large market areas. On the UNITS variable only low income is associated with high coffee purchasing. Heavy tea purchasing families again, as in the coffee data, tend to be large, but unlike the heavy coffee drinkers, they tend not to have cars, and to live in smaller market areas. Heavy consumers of beer tend to be low in income and to live in larger market areas.

The personality results on activity are relatively more stable across the four dependent variables than is the case for either brand or store behavior, but appear to be somewhat less stable across products. Looking at these results for coffee, the family that consumes a lot of coffee tends to have a husband who is high on need for intraception, and a wife who is high on needs for endurance. Intraception is a need to be analytical about oneself and others, and this finding reinforces the stereotype of the coffee drinker as an intellectual. Endurance needs in the high coffee drinking wife are needs for completion and closure.

Heavy coffee drinking families also have husbands who are low in needs for deference, order, and affiliation. The latter finding is of some interest, since to some extent it contradicts the sterotype of coffee drinkers as hearty, sociable, and friendly. On balance, the picture we get of the heavy coffee drinking family is one in which the husbands are analytical, independent, have low needs for order, and are not very friendly; the wife is a lady with strong completion needs.

The heavy tea drinking family is characterized almost exclusively by husband's personality scores. In this family the husband is high on needs for affiliation, endurance, and aggression. He's a friendly guy with strong completion needs, who isn't afraid to criticize others in public.

The family with high beer consumption has a wife with high needs for endurance (like the heavy coffee drinking families), high needs for succorance, and a husband with low needs for deference.

In summary, the relationships between personality data and consumption for coffee, tea, and beer seem useful in characterizing heavy users of these products. To some degree the findings here have contradicted the more commonly held stereotypes of the coffee and tea

Table 6–6
SELECTED RESULTS ON ACTIVITY VARIABLES

(Variables listed are those on which regression
coefficients were significant beyond the .05 level.
Sign before variable indicates direction of relationship.)

1. Coffee

ACTIV	UNITS	TRIPS	UNPTP
+HINTRA	+HINTRA	+HINTRA	
			+HSUCCR
			+WAUTON
+WENDUR	+WENDUR	+WENDUR	+WENDUR
+FAMSIZ	+FAMSIZ	+FAMSIZ	+FAMSIZ
+OWNCAR	+OWNCAR	+OWNCAR	
	+MKTSIZ		+MKTSIZ
	-HDEFER	-HDEFER	
-HORDER	-HORDER		
-HAFFIL	-HAFFIL	-HAFFIL	
		-WABASE	
	-INCOCC		

2. Tea

ATIVT	UNITS	TRIPS	UNPTP
	+HAUTON		+HAUTON
+HAFFIL	+HAFFIL	+HAFFIL	
	+HSUCCR		
		+HNURTR	
+HENDUR	+HENDUR	+HENDUR	
+HAGGRE	+HAGGRE		
		+WDEFER	
		+WORDER	
+FAMSIZ	+FAMSIZ		+FAMSIZ
	-OWNCAR	-OWNCAR	
-MKTSIZ	-MKTSIZ		-MKTSIZ

3. Beer

ACTIV	UNITS	TRIPS	UNPTP
			+WORDER
		+HEXHIB	+HEXHIB
			+WINTRA
	+WSUCCR	+WSUCCR	
			+WABASE
			+WNURTR
+WENDUR	+WENDUR	+WENDUR	
	+MKTSIZ		
	-HDEFER	-HDEFER	-HDEFER
			-HCHANG
			-WAFFIL
			-FAMSIZ
-INCOCC	-INCOCC		

drinker: the heavy coffee drinking husband turns out to be cool, detached, and analytical, and the heavy tea drinking husband is a friendly, aggressive person with high needs for closure. Heavy coffee drinking is a big-city practice, while heavy tea drinking is a small-town pattern. The husband in the high beer consuming family is low in needs for deference. The wife has high need to be taken care of by others and high needs for closure.

CONCLUSIONS

Taken altogether, these findings must be characterized as disappointing and somewhat surprising. Considering our earlier remarks on the reliability of measurement on the purchasing measures and the personality variables, we expected to account for a more substantial proportion of the variance in purchasing behavior. Given the importance attached to personality factors in the marketing literature over the past fifteen years, we expected the Edwards test to perform much better than it did. On the other hand, our findings are not qualitatively different (in terms of ability to predict) than those obtained for automobiles (Evans, 1959 and 1962), toilet paper (Advertising Research Foundation, 1963), and a number of other grocery products (Koponen, 1960) which were also based on the EPPS. Similar findings for baking products have also been reported (Ruch, 1966). We also expected our socio-economic data to predict better than they did, given the reliance placed on them in most marketing studies. Two to four percent of the variance for SES alone, and five to ten percent for the total battery must be considered surprisingly poor prediction.

This research has some obvious limitations that should be noted again here. As with all secondary analyses, the data were not collected specifically for the purposes for which we used them. This placed severe limitations on our ability to formulate and test specific hypotheses, and led us to ask general questions of the data rather than making and testing specific assertions about them. We felt it would be pretentious to do otherwise, given the inherent limitations of the data and the paucity of theoretical work in this area.

Our lack of data on environmental events is an even more severe limitation. In classic psychological terms, we are missing the stimulus part of the stimulus-organism-response prediction model. Without this, we are forced into using a trait-psychology model, where we only have data on organism (personality and SES) and response (purchasing behavior). It is clear from our results that this model is inadequate for understanding purchasing behavior, but it may be of some use to have laid this hoary antique to rest once again.

Finally, we must note that what results we have are limited to three product classes, all of them beverages. Our decision on this was partly dictated by the availability of data in sufficient quantities and also was made on the grounds that coffee, especially, is a well-researched product in other studies. While this is a limitation, we may also note that very few studies in this area deal with more than one product class.

In a sense, our findings generate more problems than they resolve. The various measures of buying behavior that were used are relatively reliable phenomena. Our sample was large and nationally distributed, and we carefully selected the best combination of predictor and dependent measures using data from the analysis sample. We know of no other study done on so large a scale, and we must conclude that our understanding of purchasing behavior is much more limited than has generally been thought.

If socio-economic and general personality characteristics are not important determinants of household buying behavior, then what variables are likely to make a difference? In order to answer this question we need to keep in mind two additional pieces of information: 1) Though reliable, our measures of buying behavior (except for store loyalty) have relatively low correlations from one product to the next; 2) A person's personality, as measured by the Edwards test, presumably reflects enduring needs of the individual, that is, needs that are "common denominators" of his behavior regardless of the nature of the problem and/or situation with which he is faced.

The presence of relatively high reliability leads us in the direction of believing that a large component of household buying behavior is systematic in nature and potentially amenable to understanding and prediction. In spite of this fact, personality and socio-economic characteristics have low correlations with buying behavior. The low intercorrelations of purchasing behavior across products provides a possible insight into this anomaly. The more stable household purchasing behavior is from one product or situation to the next, the more importance can be attached to enduring characteristics of an individual as determinants of such behavior. The logic of this argument leads us to believe that one of the most fruitful directions for future research is the study of characteristics (including attitudes, valuational criteria, physical distribution) that are idiosyncratic to both the customer and the product and not to the customer alone as in the case of general personality characteristics. In addition to obtaining measurements of attitudes, use opportunities, and marketing and physical distribution variables, it may be desirable to construct special-purpose personality measures for this kind of study. Our results do not indicate that personality variables do not predict— they clearly do—but perhaps a general-purpose test like the Edwards is not adequate to the job as a battery of instruments specifically constructed for this purpose would be.

Second, it is very clear from our results that more work needs to be done on family decision-making patterns. Husband's personality scores clearly correlate significantly with loyalty and activity variables, but how and at what point his influence is exerted remains a mystery. When such a study is done, it will probably be found that this varies considerably over products; if so, this would also help account for our low "loyalty-proneness" correlations and the low stability of our personality correlations over products.

Another line of attack for future research is suggested by the fact that our study is cross-sectional rather than longitudinal. Our purchasing behavior variables are obtained by averaging or aggregating a one-year time series of buying data for each household in the sample. While these variables do tap many of the dynamic characteristics of purchasing behavior (see Chapter III), no attempt has been made to deal with time changes, *per se*, or to relate them to changes in environmental variables. It may be that while personality characteristics are not very important determinants of average household buying behavior, as it exists at a particular point in time, they may still play a key role in predicting how different households will adjust their activity and loyalty patterns to temporal changes in the environment—e.g., advertising campaigns, changes in retail availability, entrance of new brands, shifts in reference group orientations, etc.

A program of research aimed at evaluating the effects of personality needs (and socio-economic status) on response to environmental changes would have to begin with the development of response measures that are either household-specific or are defined over small strata that are relatively homogeneous in the relevant explanatory variables. This requires both panel data on household purchases and time series data on environmental events. Frank and Massy (1965), Massy and Frank (1965), Duhammel (1966), Claycamp and Massy (1966), and Frank and Massy (forthcoming in 1968) have analyzed differences in the response to promotional efforts of households with different socio-economic characteristics. Unfortunately, the panel data used in these studies do not include measures of personality.[1]

In spite of the obvious limitations of our study, many of the relationships we found do exhibit reasonable stability. They add an increment to our knowledge about household-to-household variations in time-averaged purchasing behavior. For example, endurance needs turned out to be a significant correlate of brand and story loyalty, and we believe our two-factor interpretation of the personality bases of loyalty will stand up with further study. Our interpretation of the affiliation-deference low loyalty pattern as susceptibility to influence is also an interesting topic for future work. Personality data seem especially stable and useful in interpreting high and low consumption patterns over the three product classes studied. Nevertheless, we feel this study is definitive in showing that temporal averages of purchasing behavior are measures not predictable in any simple and direct way from personality and socio-economic status variables.

If we have rolled out a cannon to shoot a mouse in this research, we can take some comfort in the discovery that the mouse turned out to be more elusive than was thought. The brute force of the cannon will have to be traded for a much more differentiated set of concepts and instruments; by itself, the best available cannon of modern multivariate statistics only hit seven percent of the mouse.

NOTES

All of these studies are based on data for households residing in one metropolitan area. This permits a relatively unambiguous determination of the time series for relevant promotional variables — either from the panel itself or through supplementary field work. We considered the possibility that environmental time series might be developed for the (national) J. Walter Thompson panel, which provided the data base for the present study, but concluded that such a program was not feasible, given available resources.

APPENDICES

APPENDIX A

TABLES

Table A–1.1
COFFEE VALIDATION SAMPLE REGRESSION COEFFICIENTS AND T-RATIOS FOR ACTIVITY VARIABLES*
(1282 Households)

	ACTIV	UNITS	TRIPS	UNPTP
HDEFER	-3.32	-1.81	-1.68[a]	.03
	(1.41)	(1.72)	(2.05)	(.04)
HORDER	-5.78[a]	-2.16[a]	-1.26	-.23
	(2.48)	(2.07)	(1.54)	(.34)
HEXHIB	-1.57	-.44	-.60	.44
	(.60)	(.38)	(.66)	(.59)
HAUTON	-.91	-.06	-1.05	1.05
	(.41)	(.06)	(1.33)	(1.66)
HAFFIL	-6.63[a]	-2.27	-1.81[a]	.05
	(2.52)	(1.93)	(1.97)	(.07)
HINTRA	4.92[a]	2.28[a]	1.40	.62
	(2.12)	(2.20)	(1.73)	(.94)
HSUCCR	.75	1.33	-.21	1.27
	(.32)	(1.25)	(.25)	(1.90)
HABASE	-1.55	-.43	-.01	-.29
	(.63)	(-.39)	(.02)	(.42)
HNURTR	-3.25	-.93	-1.09	.14
	(1.18)	(.76)	(1.13)	(.18)
HCHANG	-2.83	-.31	-.69	.43
	(1.25)	(.30)	(.87)	(.68)
HENDUR	2.63	1.16	.51	.45
	(1.06)	(1.05)	(.59)	(.64)

128

Table A-1.1 (Continued)

	ACTIV	UNITS	TRIPS	UNPTP
HAGGRE	-3.06	.10	-.86	1.05
	(1.23)	(.09)	(.99)	(1.49)
WDEFER	2.46	1.53	.88	.48
	(.94)	(1.31)	(.97)	(.66)
WORDER	-.98	.03	-.14	.33
	(.40)	(.03)	(.17)	(.48)
WEXHIB	2.45	1.30	.36	.67
	(.94)	(1.12)	(.40)	(.92)
WAUTON	.90	1.54	-.60	1.99[a]
	(.40)	(1.52)	(.76)	(3.13)
WAFFIL	1.38	.73	.61	.10
	(.55)	(.65)	(.70)	(.14)
WINTRA	-.17	.60	-.20	.54
	(.07)	(.56)	(.24)	(.81)
WSUCCR	1.14	.09	-.56	.53
	(.45)	(.07)	(.63)	(.75)
WABASE	-2.50	-.46	-1.36	.88
	(1.11)	(.45)	(1.72)	(1.38)
WNURTR	-.40	.23	-.50	.82
	(.16)	(.21)	(.57)	(1.17)
WCHANG	.58	-.61	.05	-.65
	(.25)	(.58)	(.06)	(.99)
WENDUR	6.84[a]	4.45[a]	1.43	2.25[a]
	(2.93)	(4.26)	(1.76)	(3.42)
WAGGRE	1.66	1.08	.41	.59
	(.61)	(.89)	(.43)	(.78)
WOMAGE	.15	.65	-.07	.56
	(.13)	(1.31)	(.18)	(1.79)
FAMSIZE	35.71[a]	18.87[a]	10.20[a]	6.46[a]
	(4.54)	(5.36)	(3.71)	(2.92)
OWNCAR	86.75[a]	29.77	26.57[a]	-7.21
	(2.28)	(1.74)	(1.99)	(.67)
MKTSIZ	.88	.56	.09	.33
	(1.29)	(1.85)	(.38)	(1.74)
IWCOCC	-53.62	-60.78	-27.48	-28.04
	(.74)	(1.88)	(1.09)	(1.38)
F-total	2.69[a]	2.16[a]	2.10[a]	3.04a
F-ad	1.61[a]	1.64[a]	1.31	2.30a
R^2	.059	.048	.047	.066

*All coefficients transformed by multiplying by 10^{-2}.
a Significant at the 5% level.

Table A-1.2

TEA VALIDATION SAMPLE REGRESSION COEFFICIENTS AND T-RATIOS FOR ACTIVITY VARIABLES*

(899 Households)

	ATTVU	ATIVT	UNITS	TRIPS	UNPTP
HDEFER	-1.53	-.97	.02	-.63	1.70
	(.50)	(.40)	(.01)	(.15)	(1.35)
HORDER	-1.09	1.55	1.07	.69	-1.21
	(.36)	(.65)	(.57)	(.95)	(.98)
HEXHIB	.04	2.68	1.10	1.29	-2.21
	(.01)	(.98)	(.50)	(1.54)	(1.55)
HAUTON	4.21	1.89	3.54	.29	2.48[a]
	(1.42)	(.81)	(1.90)	(.41)	(2.03)
HAFFIL	7.29[a]	4.89	4.35[a]	1.57	1.14
	(2.17)	(1.84)	(2.05)	(1.93)	(.82)
HINTRA	-.98	2.48	-.27	-.20	-1.88
	(.31)	(1.01)	(.14)	(.26)	(1.46)
HSUCCR	4.98	1.59	3.17	.61	1.63
	(1.64)	(.66)	(1.66)	(.82)	(1.30)
HABASE	.12	-.35	-1.26	-.35	-1.76
	(.04)	(.14)	(.62)	(.45)	(1.32)
HNURTR	3.52	5.99[a]	3.66	1.88[a]	.77
	(.97)	(2.08)	(1.60)	(2.13)	(.51)
HCHANG	-2.83	-.49	-.32	-.20	-.73
	(.91)	(.20)	(.16)	(.27)	(.56)
HENDUR	9.94[a]	8.18[a]	5.39[a]	2.45[a]	.98
	(3.09)	(3.21)	(2.66)	(3.13)	(.74)
HAGGRE	6.65	5.66[a]	3.73	1.09	1.33
	(1.91)	(2.18)	(1.81)	(1.37)	(.98)
WDEFER	2.31	3.04	1.47	.15	-1.15
	(.67)	(1.12)	(.68)	(.18)	(.11)
WORDER	.07	3.20	2.57	1.38	.15
	(.02)	(1.22)	(1.23)	(1.71)	(.11)
WEXHIB	1.16	1.85	-.71	-.22	.48
	(.34)	(.69)	(.33)	(.26)	(.34)
WAUTON	-.40	1.21	.54	.64	-.89
	(.14)	(.52)	(.29)	(.90)	(.74)
WAFFIL	-2.22	-.87	.17	.51	-.25
	(.68)	(.33)	(.08)	(.64)	(.18)
WINTRA	-.78	1.95	.54	1.25	-1.12
	(.24)	(.77)	(.27)	(1.60)	(.84)
WSUCCR	2.80	1.84	.72	.47	-.19
	(.82)	(.68)	(.34)	(.56)	(.14)
WABASE	-1.46	-.15	-.93	.01	-.97
	(.48)	(.06)	(.49)	(.02)	(.77)
WNURTR	3.18	4.80	1.82	.39	-.08
	(.93)	(1.76)	(.84)	(.47)	(.06)
WCHANG	1.37	-.76	-.23	.43	.13
	(.45)	(.31)	(.12)	(.58)	(.10)

Table A-1.2 (Continued)

	ATTVU	ATIVT	UNITS	TRIPS	UNPTP
WENDUR	2.47	3.13	.36	.36	-.06
	(.79)	(1.26)	(.18)	(.47)	(.04)
WAGGRE	.02	-.00	-.35	-.53	0.50
	(.00)	(.00)	(.15)	(.58)	(.32)
WOMAGE	-1.88	-2.84^a	-.81	-.89^a	.32
	(1.34)	(2.57)	(.92)	(2.62)	(.54)
FAMSIZE	33.91^a	20.37^a	30.49^a	3.71	10.77^a
	(3.15)	(2.39)	(4.48)	(1.41)	(2.41)
OWNCAR	-66.76	-86.86^a	-48.66	-19.58	-6.23
	(1.52)	(2.49)	(1.75)	(1.83)	(.34)
MKTSIZ	-2.21^a	-.72	-.99	.09	-.84^a
	(2.46)	(1.00)	(1.75)	(.41)	(2.26)
INCOCC	-126.38	-116.37	-46.00	-10.97	36.33
	(1.41)	(1.64)	(.81)	(.50)	(.98)
F-total	2.18^a	2.42^a	2.31^a	1.74^a	1.34
F-ad	1.18	.57	1.19	1.46^a	.94
R^2	.068	.075	.072	.055	.043

*All coefficients transformed by multiplying by 10^{-2}.
[a]Significant at the 5% level.

Table A-1.3

BEER VALIDATION SAMPLE REGRESSION COEFFICIENTS AND T-RATIOS FOR ACTIVITY VARIABLES*

(485 Households)

	ACTIV	UNITS	TRIPS	UNPTP
HDEFER	-9.61	-11.05	-4.11	-3.13
	(1.58)	(1.63)	(1.91)	(1.75)
HORDER	-6.83	-7.08	-.33	-.98
	(1.20)	(1.12)	(.16)	(.59)
HEXHIB	7.24	12.13	1.69	1.12
	(1.08)	(1.63)	(.71)	(.57)
HAUTON	-3.36	-.24	-1.10	-1.01
	(.61)	(.04)	(.56)	(.62)
HAFFIL	.84	-2.22	.47	.58
	(.12)	(.28)	(.19)	(.28)
HINTRA	-.95	3.68	1.34	-2.08
	(.16)	(.54)	(.62)	(1.16)
HSUCCR	-3.41	-6.21	-1.67	-1.69
	(.55)	(.89)	(.75)	(.92)
HABASE	2.16	5.33	1.69	-.48
	(.35)	(.78)	(.77)	(.26)
HNURTR	3.93	5.46	-.36	-.77
	(.57)	(.72)	(.15)	(.38)
HCHANG	-2.91	-9.36	-.13	-3.80[a]
	(.50)	(1.43)	(.06)	(2.19)
HENDUR	7.76	-2.26	-1.12	1.15
	(1.25)	(.33)	(.51)	(.63)
HAGGRE	.46	-.45	-1.13	-.21
	(.08)	(.07)	(.52)	(.11)
WDEFER 1.0 0.0	3.88	6.17	2.61	.60
	(.58)	(.82)	(1.09)	(.30)
WORDER	-.51	5.33	-2.20	4.37[a]
	(.08)	(.77)	(.99)	(2.39)
WEXHIB	-2.98	-5.74	-2.90	6.87a
	(.47)	(.81)	(1.28)	(3.66)
WAUTON	4.97	4.26	1.80	-.43
	(.86)	(.66)	(.88)	(.25)
WAFFIL	-5.49	-2.99	1.49	-2.93
	(.89)	(.43)	(.67)	(1.61)
WINTRA	3.65	9.13	3.23	2.86
	(.63)	(1.41)	(1.56)	(1.66)
WSUCCR	7.23	12.06	4.11	.39
	(1.20)	(1.80)	(1.93)	(.22)
WABASE	-1.43	2.56	.34	4.12[a]
	(.26)	(.42)	(.18)	(2.56)

Table A-1.3 (Continued)

	ACTIV	UNITS	TRIPS	UNPTP
WNURTR	7.02	8.65	.20	3.27
	(1.10)	(1.21)	(.09)	(1.73)
WCHANG	-2.78	6.21	-1.03	-.43
	(.48)	(.96)	(.50)	(.25)
WENDUR	9.97	11.44	-.46[a]	1.72
	(1.79)	(1.84)	(2.34)	(1.05)
WAGGRE	-3.87	5.41	1.09	3.03
	(.57)	(.71)	(.45)	(1.51)
WOMAGE	-1.42	-4.62	-.80	-.39
	(.50)	(1.46)	(.79)	(.47)
FAMSIZE	-27.33	-33.18	-7.86	-9.44
	(1.41)	(1.54)	(1.14)	(1.65)
OWNCAR	-74.69	-58.94	-56.93	-7.67
	(.74)	(.52)	(1.59)	(.26)
MKTSIZ	2.74	2.23	1.24[a]	.20
	(1.55)	(1.14)	(1.98)	(.38)
INCOCC	-503.89[a]	-249.10	-110.69	·76.20
	(2.68)	(1.19)	(1.66)	(1.38)
F-total	1.25	1.26	1.25	1.76[a]
F-ad	.80	1.25	1.07	1.87[a]
R^2	.074	.074	.074	.101

*All coefficients transformed by multiplying by 10^{-2}
[a]Significant at the 5% level.

Table A—2.1
COFFEE VALIDATION SAMPLE REGRESSION COEFFICIENTS AND T-RATIOS FOR BRAND BEHAVIOR VARIABLES*
(1282 Households)

	LOYAL	BRLOY	BRAND	SHILB	BCONS	SNDIB	lSNDlB
HDEFER	-14.06[a]	-14.99[a]	.90	-.49[a]	-2.03	.81	.53
	(2.52)	(3.25)	(1.89)	(2.44)	(1.23)	(.81)	(.76)
HORDER	-.20	2.77	-.83	.12	-2.56	-.54	-.55
	(.04)	(.60)	(1.77)	(.62)	(1.57)	(.54)	(.79)
HEXHIB	3.94	.94	-.29	-.06	.58	-.09	-.43
	(.64)	(.18)	(.55)	(.29)	(.32)	(.08)	(.55)
HAUTON	6.52	2.61	-.30	.01	.15	1.37	-1.24
	(1.22)	(.59)	(.65)	(.03)	(.10)	(1.43)	(1.85)
HAFFIL	4.01	2.28	-.48	.14	-4.71[a]	2.34[a]	-1.29
	(.64)	(.44)	(.91)	(.62)	(2.56)	(2.08)	(1.64)
HINTRA	4.36	3.29	.28	-.06	4.48[a]	-1.53	1.02
	(.79)	(.72)	(.61)	(.29)	(2.77)	(1.55)	(1.48)
HSUCCR	7.51	6.42	-.15	-.04	4.39[a]	-2.41[a]	.23
	(1.33)	(1.37)	(.32)	(.19)	(2.64)	(2.37)	(.32)
HABASE	7.42	6.20	-.27	.17	-1.18	-.74	.03
	(1.28)	(1.29)	(.55)	(.82)	(.69)	(.71)	(.04)
HNURTR	4.79	3.95	-.85	.31	-2.36	2.26	-.58
	(.74)	(.73)	(1.52)	(1.31)	(1.23)	(1.72)	(.70)
HCHANG	2.29	3.03	-.34	.06	.47	-1.06	.25
	(.43)	(.69)	(.75)	(.30)	(.30)	(1.10)	(.36)
HENDUR	12.03[a]	7.12	-.63	.11	1.97	-.21	.02
	(2.05)	(1.47)	(1.27)	(.51)	(1.14)	(.20)	(.02)
HAGGRE	5.32	3.26	-.11	.22	-1.48	1.43	-.49
	(.90)	(.67)	(.22)	(1.05)	(.85)	(1.34)	(.65)
WDEFER	11.00	11.49[a]	-.75	.45[a]	2.24	-.75	-.25
	(1.78)	(2.25)	(1.43)	(2.01)	(1.23)	(.68)	(.32)
WORDER	.20	-.07	-.33	.13	.01	.43	.11
	(.03)	(.01)	(.66)	(.61)	(.00)	(.42)	(.15)
WEXHIB	4.93	2.88	-.11	.02	2.67	-1.07	-.01
	(.80)	(.57)	(.21)	(.08)	(1.48)	(.97)	(.02)
WAUTON	9.52	7.48	-.75	.21	5.27[a]	-1.33	.01
	(1.78)	(1.69)	(1.64)	(1.08)	(3.34)	(1.38)	(.01)
WAFFIL	4.57	2.52	-.09	.03	.58	-1.27	.38
	(.77)	(.51)	(.18)	(.14)	(.33)	(1.19)	(.51)
WINTRA	4.62	4.68	-.56	.10	1.68	-.01	.74
	(.82)	(1.00)	(1.16)	(.48)	(1.01)	(.01)	(1.05)
WSUCCR	12.03[a]	8.62	-.89	.29	2.06	-.42	-.78
	(2.01)	(1.74)	(1.75)	(1.33)	(1.16)	(.38)	(1.02)
WABASE	7.17	5.10	-.86	.22	1.42	.51	-.74
	(1.34)	(1.15)	(1.89)	(1.16)	(.90)	(.53)	(1.09)
WNURTR	-3.01	-1.74	-.11	-.14	2.78	-.73	.05
	(.51)	(.36)	(.21)	(.64)	(1.59)	(.69)	(.06)
WCHANG	-9.99	-6.77	.59	-.16	-1.24	-.71	-.51
	(1.81)	(1.48)	(1.25)	(.81)	(.76)	(.72)	(.73)
WENDUR	8.18	6.71	.02	.15	7.71[a]	-2.52[a]	.60
	(1.48)	(1.47)	(.04)	(.73)	(4.72)	(2.53)	(.85)

Table A-2.1 (Continued)

	LOYAL	BRLOY	BRAND	SHILB	BCONS	SNDIB	|SNDIB|
WAGGRE	1.03	2.55	-.44	.16	1.59	-.73	-.34
	(.16)	(.48)	(.81)	(.68)	(.84)	(.63)	(.41)
WOMAGE	-3.97	-3.27	.32	-.12	.31	.78	-.21
	(1.50)	(1.49)	(1.40)	(1.20)	(.39)	(1.63)	(.63)
FAMSIZ	24.62	21.34	.10	.18	26.24^a	-2.60	2.37
	(1.32)	(1.38)	(.06)	(.26)	(4.78)	(.77)	(1.00)
OWNCAR	-27.79	-53.97	14.83	-5.43	23.71	.73	13.99
	(.31)	(.72)	(1.93)	(1.67)	(.89)	(.04)	(1.22)
MKTSIZ	-4.36^a	-3.22^a	.71^a	-.20^a	.45	-.05	.13
	(2.70)	(2.41)	(5.20)	(3.45)	(.96)	(.16)	(.63)
INCOCC	-486.48^a	-455.74^a	28.04	-14.84^a	-46.02	-33.33	-4.53
	(2.85)	(3.23)	(1.93)	(2.41)	(.91)	(1.09)	(.21)
F-total	2.44^a	2.42^a	3.13^a	2.05^a	3.25^a	1.56^a	.99
F-ad	1.62^a	1.63^a	1.39	1.09	3.02^a	1.41	.88
R^2	.054	.053	.068	.045	.070	.035	.022

*All coefficients transformed by multiplying by 10^{-2}.
[a]Significant at the 5% level.

Table A–2.2
TEA VALIDATION SAMPLE REGRESSION COEFFICIENTS AND T-RATIOS FOR BRAND BEHAVIOR VARIABLES*
(899 Households)

	LOYAL	BRLOY	BRAND	SHILB	BCONS	SNDIB	|SNDIB|
HDEFER	-6.02	-5.60	.40	-.16	-.08	2.33[a]	.70
	(.87)	(1.03)	(.80)	(.67)	(.05)	(2.42)	(1.03)
HORDER	-10.18	-8.87	.76	-.38	1.10	-.36	.18
	(1.50)	(1.67)	(1.55)	(1.64)	(.71)	(.38)	(.27)
HEXHIB	-6.50	-7.54	.83	-.64[a]	1.53	-1.33	.69
	(.83)	(1.23)	(1.47)	(2.36)	(.85)	(1.22)	(.90)
HAUTON	2.59	-1.27	.49	-.10	1.37	-.30	.96
	(.39)	(1.24)	(1.03)	(.42)	(.89)	(.32)	(1.48)
HAFFIL	11.06	7.71	-.88	.30	2.89	-1.15	.12
	(1.45)	(1.29)	(1.60)	(1.14)	(1.65)	(1.08)	(.17)
HINTRA	2.89	-4.42	.40	-.21	-1.17	.06	.43
	(.41)	(.80)	(1.79)	(.86)	(.73)	(.06)	(.63)
HSUCCR	4.44	2.62	.36	-.02	.79	-.39	.87
	(.64)	(.49)	(1.74)	(.09)	(.50)	(.41)	(1.29)
HABASE	7.57	3.43	-.38	.09	-.72	-1.32	-1.23
	(1.04)	(.60)	(.72)	(.37)	(.43)	(1.29)	(1.74)
HNURTR	-2.00	-1.31	.12	.02	1.59	.84	-.39
	(.24)	(.20)	(.20)	(.07)	(.84)	(.73)	(.49)
HCHANG	-10.31	-9.84	.93	-.48[a]	.16	.12	.65
	(1.46)	(1.78)	(1.83)	(1.97)	(.10)	(.13)	(.94)
HENDUR	18.36[a]	10.71	-.22	.15	2.05	-1.31	.62
	(2.51)	(1.88)	(.41)	(.60)	(1.23)	(1.28)	(.87)
HAGGRE	10.87	5.88	-.34	-.04	3.76	-.78	.00
	(1.47)	(1.01)	(.64)	(.14)	(2.22)	(.75)	(.00)
WDEFER	7.09	5.89[a]	-.64	.45	-1.02	-1.17	-.20
	(.91)	(1.97)	(1.15)	(1.66)	(.57)	(1.08)	(.26)
WORDER	-13.68	-11.37	1.34[a]	-.50	.78	.78	.76
	(1.82)	(1.94)	(2.47)	(1.95)	(.45)	(.74)	(1.04)
WEXHIB	7.01	7.06	-1.15	.51	-.73	.30	-.86
	(.92)	(1.18)	(2.10)	(1.94)	(.42)	(.28)	(1.15)
WAUTON	.16	1.08	.01	.12	.04	-.11	.90
	(.02)	(1.21)	(.01)	(.50)	(.03)	(.12)	(1.40)
WAFFIL	-6.72	2.32	-.02	.19	-3.61[a]	1.40	-.98
	(.90)	(1.40)	(.04)	(.75)	(2.11)	(1.35)	(1.35)
WINTRA	-3.92	3.56	.58	-.10	-.44	.62	.21
	(.54)	(.62)	(1.12)	(.39)	(.26)	(.61)	(.30)
WSUCCR	9.75	8.16	-.83	.35	-1.06	-1.80	-.74
	(1.26)	(1.35)	(.150)	(1.30)	(.60)	(.17)	(.98)
WABASE	2.50	-1.34	-.14	.03	-.87	1.47	.33
	(.36)	(1.25)	(.28)	(.14)	(.55)	(1.53)	(.50)
WNURTR	2.76	-.11	-.05	-.02	1.58	-1.21	.24
	(.35)	(.02)	(.10)	(.06)	(.88)	(1.11)	(.32)
WCHANG	-.85	1.86	.07	-.22	1.16	.34	-.47
	(.12)	(1.34)	(.14)	(.92)	(.73)	(.35)	(.69)
WENDUR	10.41	8.32	-.89	.36	.26	-1.07	-.56
	(1.46)	(1.49)	(1.74)	(1.45)	(.16)	(1.07)	(.81)

Table A-2.2 (Continued)

	LOYAL	BRLOY	BRAND	SHILB	BCONS	SNDIB	ISNDIBI
WAGGRE	-3.02	.31	-.57	.28	-1.23	.26	-1.70[a]
	(.36)	(1.05)	(.94)	(.95)	(.64)	(.22)	(2.08)
WOMAGE	-4.74	-3.46	.15	-.14	.90	.71	-.42
	(1.49)	(1.40)	(.66)	(1.27)	(1.24)	(1.61)	(1.36)
FAMSIZ	18.92	.44	.77	.21	6.12	-2.22	-.53
	(.77)	(.02)	(.44)	(.25)	(1.09)	(.65)	(.22)
OWNCAR	-86.05	-66.99	.66	-1.16	-15.61	7.26	-27.00[a]
	(.86)	(.86)	(.09)	(.34)	(.68)	(.52)	(2.78)
MKTSIZ	-5.76	-3.21[a]	.40[a]	-.14	.24	-.07	.04
	(2.82)	(2.01)	(2.74)	(1.94)	(.52)	(.26)	(.22)
INCOCC	-362.68	-233.09	28.29	-10.89	14.92	48.01	29.44
	(1.79)	(1.47)	(1.94)	(1.56)	(.32)	(1.70)	(1.49)
F-total	1.78[a]	1.38	1.70	1.46	.88	.94	1.16
F-ad	1.19	1.14	1.61	1.30	1.40	.81	1.00
R^2	.056	.044	.054	.047	.028	.030	.037

*All coefficients transformed by multiplying by 10^{-2}
[a]Significant at the 5% level.

Table A-2.3
BEER VALIDATION SAMPLE REGRESSION COEFFICIENTS
AND T-RATIOS FOR BRAND BEHAVIOR VARIABLES*
(485 Households)

	LOYAL	BRLOY	BRAND	SHILB	BCONS	SNDIB	ISNDIBI
HDEFER	-2.36	3.48	-.15	.23	-5.98	1.58	-2.29
	(.31)	(.60)	(.19)	(.65)	(1.75)	(.74)	(1.31)
HORDER	-11.85	-4.77	.92	-.16	-5.47	-3.20	1.84
	(1.63)	(.88)	(1.23)	(.50)	(1.71)	(1.59)	(1.12)
HEXHIB	10.60	4.09	.35	.05	5.40	-1.68	1.05
	(1.24)	(.64)	(.40)	(.14)	(1.43)	(.71)	(.55)
HAUTON	-5.40	-3.77	.19	-.17	-2.13	.25	-.54
	(.76)	(.71)	(.26)	(.55)	(.68)	(.13)	(.34)
HAFFIL	3.41	3.98	-.93	.27	2.34	-2.89	3.18
	(.38)	(.60)	(1.00)	(.68)	(.59)	(1.15)	(1.56)
HINTRA	-8.81	-8.11	.63	-.35	-.64	.22	-.54
	(1.14)	(1.39)	(.78)	(1.00)	(.19)	(.10)	(.31)
HSUCCR	-.27	7.10	-.95	.51	-3.50	1.06	-1.45
	(.03)	(1.19)	(1.15)	(1.43)	(.99)	(.48)	(.82)
HABASE	.72	-1.66	1.25	-.54	1.64	-.19	2.73
	(.09)	(.28)	(1.53)	(1.54)	(.47)	(.08)	(1.54)
HNURTR	6.32	4.66	-.55	.46	-4.24	.73	-3.56
	(.72)	(.71)	(.61)	(1.16)	(1.10)	(.30)	(1.82)
HCHANG	-2.16	-.77	.55	-.16	.08	-1.76	.57
	(.29)	(.14)	(.71)	(.47)	(.02)	(.84)	(.34)
HENDUR	15.66	15.05[a]	-2.09[a]	1.00[a]	3.83	-.39	1.01
	(1.98)	(2.54)	(2.54)	(2.81)	(1.09)	(.18)	(.57)
HAGGRE	-2.51	-.21	-.30	.33	-2.64	-1.25	-16.21
	(.32)	(.04)	(.38)	(.95)	(.77)	(.58)	(.65)
WDEFER	1.80	-4.51	.87	-.28	2.29	.46	.72
	(.21)	(.70)	(.98)	(.73)	(.60)	(.19)	(.37)
WORDER	7.54	8.23	-1.25	.47	.04	4.55[a]	-4.27[a]
	(.95)	(1.39)	(1.52)	(1.33)	(.01)	(2.07)	(2.40)
WEXHIB	3.90	7.80	-1.31	.22	2.39	3.07	-2.32
	(.48)	(1.28)	(1.56)	(.60)	(.67)	(1.38)	(1.28)
WAUTON	5.87	2.81	-1.19	.54	2.36	-.73	1.29
	(.80)	(.51)	(1.56)	(1.63)	(.73)	(.86)	(.78)
WAFFIL	-10.74	-7.66	.72	-.36	-3.27	-1.05	-.15
	(1.36)	(1.30)	(.88)	(1.01)	(.94)	(.48)	(.08)
WINTRA	-3.82	-8.64	1.59[a]	-.44	4.00	-.88	1.33
	(.51)	(1.55)	(2.06)	(1.31)	(1.22)	(.43)	(.79)
WSUCCR	.10	-6.46	.71	-.38	4.89	-4.62[a]	1.15
	(.01)	(1.13)	(.90)	(1.09)	(1.45)	(2.19)	(.67)
WABASE	-5.47	-5.44	.34	-.07	-1.78	1.46	-.18
	(.79)	(1.05)	(.47)	(.21)	(.58)	(.76)	(.11)
WNURTR	14.00	10.40	-1.84[a]	.61	7.54[a]	-1.27	1.29
	(1.71)	(1.70)	(2.17)	(1.66)	(2.09)	(.56)	(.70)
WCHANG	-4.55	-1.09	.89	-.30	.81	-3.82	1.39
	(.61)	(.20)	(1.15)	(.89)	(.25)	(1.87)	(.84)
WENDUR	6.10	-1.24	-.11	.02	3.72	-2.35	2.88
	(.86)	(.23)	(.14)	(.07)	(1.19)	(1.20)	(1.81)

Table A-2.3 (Continued)

	LOYAL	BRLOY	BRAND	SHILB	BCONS	SNDIB	ISNDIBI
WAGGRE	-9.52	-4.02	.49	.06	-.77	-1.37	.94
	(1.10)	(.62)	(.55)	(.16)	(.20)	(.57)	(.48)
WOMAGE	-.46	.71	-.35	-.05	-.02	-.26	.06
	(.13)	(.26)	(.94)	(.33)	(.01)	(.25)	(.07)
FAMSIZ	-25.32	-4.86	.54	-.75	-18.21	6.26	-5.66
	(1.02)	(.26)	(.21)	(.68)	(1.67)	(.90)	(1.01)
OWNCAR	13.65	125.86	-8.77	2.53	-80.35	12.82	-4.07
	(.11)	(1.30)	(.66)	(.44)	(1.41)	(.35)	(.14)
MKTSIZ	1.91	-1.10	.19	-.13	1.97[a]	-1.67	1.22[a]
	(.85)	(.65)	(.81)	(1.26)	(1.98)	(2.68)	(2.40)
INCOCC	-739.33[a]	-354.91[a]	40.80	-20.13	-216.21[a]	-2.78	6.48
	(3.09)	(1.98)	(1.65)	(1.88)	(2.04)	(.14)	(.12)
F-total	1.41	1.43	1.83[a]	1.61[a]	1.34	1.35	1.11
F-ad	.71	1.27	1.64[a]	1.41	.97	1.19	1.04
R^2	.083	.083	.105	.093	.079	.080	.066

*All coefficients transformed by multiplying 10^{-2}.
[a]Significant at the 5% level.

Table A–3.1
COFFEE VALIDATION SAMPLE REGRESSION COEFFICIENTS AND T-RATIOS FOR STORE BEHAVIOR VARIABLES*
(1282 Households)

	STLOY	STORE	SHILS	PUNID	SNDIS	|SNDIS|
HDEFER	-3.42	-.25	.07	.77[a]	1.00	-.07
	(.90)	(.67)	(.41)	(3.19)	(1.16)	(.10)
HORDER	-3.73	.15	-.25	-.11	-1.31	-.22
	(.99)	(.41)	(1.42)	(.46)	(1.52)	(.32)
HEXHIB	5.17	-.49	.23	.12	-1.03	-.24
	(1.23)	(1.21)	(1.19)	(.44)	(1.08)	(.31)
HAUTON	7.31[a]	-.80[a]	.30	.42	-.14	-1.17
	(2.01)	(2.27)	(1.76)	(1.80)	(.16)	(1.78)
HAFFIL	4.14	-.43	.22	.45	-.62	-1.43
	(.97)	(1.04)	(1.12)	(1.68)	(.64)	(1.87)
HINTRA	2.42	-.14	.08	-.20	-.78	.05
	(.65)	(.39)	(.46)	(.83)	(.86)	(.08)
HSUCCR	3.45	-.17	.01	.22	-1.06	.45
	(.90)	(.45)	(.05)	(.92)	(1.22)	(.65)
HABASE	4.28	-.06	.06	.20	-.03	-.07
	(1.08)	(.17)	(.31)	(.79)	(.03)	(.10)
HNURTR	2.98	-.59	.17	-.09	.11	-.62
	(.67)	(1.37)	(.82)	(.31)	(.11)	(.77)
HCHANG	-.31	.20	-.15	.12	-.35	.13
	(.09)	(.58)	(.90)	(.50)	(.42)	(.20)
HENDUR	10.34[a]	-.79[a]	.38[a]	.01	-.36	.28
	(2.59)	(2.05)	(2.07)	(.04)	(.40)	(.38)
HAGGRE	4.66	-.40	.31	.27	1.61	-.97
	(1.16)	(1.02)	(1.68)	(1.03)	(1.76)	(1.34)
WDEFER	2.91	.04	.01	-.47	-1.05	-.35
	(.69)	(.10)	(.04)	(1.76)	(1.10)	(.46)
WORDER	.40	-.15	.04	-.00	.81	.25
	(.10)	(.39)	(.20)	(.03)	(.90)	(.35)
WEXHIB	4.07	-.34	.15	.23	-.78	-.67
	(.97)	(.85)	(.76)	(.88)	(.82)	(.89)
WAUTON	5.27	-.51	.09	.10	-.75	-.10
	(1.44)	(1.46)	(.53)	(.44)	(.91)	(.15)
WAFFIL	4.21	-.07	.09	.28	-.58	.36
	(1.04)	(.17)	(.45)	(1.10)	(.64)	(.50)
WINTRA	1.29	.00	-.05	.26	-.13	-.25
	(.33)	(.01)	(.29)	(1.08)	(.15)	(.37)
WSUCCR	8.36[a]	-.65	.27	-.03	-.29	-.69
	(2.05)	(1.65)	(1.42)	(.11)	(.31)	(.93)
WABASE	4.94	-.43	.12	.31	-.62	-.55
	(1.35)	(1.23)	(.69)	(1.34)	(.75)	(.84)
WNURTR	-3.07	.19	-.13	-.28	.15	-.30
	(.76)	(.49)	(.66)	(1.08)	(.16)	(.42)
WCHANG	-7.46[a]	.37	-.31	.61[a]	-.83	.25
	(1.98)	(1.01)	(1.79)	(2.56)	(.97)	(.37)

Table A-3.1 (Continued)

	STLOY	STORE	SHILS	PUNID	SNDIS	|SNDIS|
WENDUR	3.87	-.27	.12	.07	-2.57[a]	.43
	(1.03)	(.73)	(.67)	(.29)	(3.00)	(.63)
WAGGRE	-1.79	.24	-.23	-.03	-.19	-.12
	(.41)	(.57)	(1.15)	(.10)	(.17)	(.15)
WOMAGE	-2.31	.14	-.03	.16	.72	-.06
	(1.28)	(.78)	(.40)	(1.38)	(1.75)	(.17)
FAMSIZ	10.05	-.31	.39	-1.45	-4.77	1.85
	(.79)	(.25)	(.67)	(1.80)	(1.65)	(.80)
OWNCAR	23.43	4.27	1.69	4.25	-16.93	17.85
	(.38)	(.72)	(.59)	(1.09)	(1.21)	(1.60)
MKTSIZ	-3.03[a]	.44[a]	-.13[a]	.10	-.11	.58[a]
	(2.76)	(4.11)	(2.62)	(1.46)	(1.44)	(2.91)
INCOCC	-202.52	1.01	-1.70	1.57	37.60	-17.48
	(1.74)	(.09)	(.32)	(.21)	(1.42)	(.83)
F-total	2.05[a]	1.97[a]	1.50	1.68[a]	1.25	1.09
F-ad	1.47[a]	1.04	1.58[a]	1.45	1.07	.57
R^2	.045	.044	.034	.038	.028	.025

*All coefficients transformed by multiplying by 10^{-2}.

[a]Significant at the 5% level.

Table A—3.2
TEA VALIDATION SAMPLE REGRESSION COEFFICIENTS AND T-RATIOS FOR STORE BEHAVIOR VARIABLES*
(899 Households)

	STLOY	STORE	SHILS	PUNID	SNDIS	|SNDIS|
HDEFER	-1.38	.01	.07	.55a	1.15	-.17
	(.31)	(.03)	(.33)	(1.98)	(1.43)	(.26)
HORDER	-6.01	.37	-.22	-.00	-.65	.74
	(1.37)	(.86)	(1.03)	(.01)	(.83)	(1.17)
HEXHIB	-2.66	.00	-.02	.07	.44	.40
	(.53)	(.00)	(.08)	(.23)	(.48)	(.55)
HAUTON	3.67	-.26	.19	-.01	-.09	.33
	(.85)	(.60)	(.91)	(.03)	(.11)	(.53)
HAFFIL	3.49	.12	.08	-.64a	-.98	.23
	(.71)	(.26)	(.35)	(2.09)	(1.10)	(.32)
HINTRA	1.65	-.12	.23	-.20	.89	.17
	(.36)	(.27)	(1.02)	(.71)	(1.09)	(.27)
HSUCCR	.68	.02	.14	.15	.76	-.22
	(.15)	(.04)	(.64)	(.55)	(.95)	(.34)
HABASE	8.59	-.57	.39	-.32	-.15	.34
	(1.83)	(1.24)	(1.70)	(1.08)	(.18)	(.51)
HNURTR	-4.83	-.09	-.24	-.37	-1.86	.98
	(.91)	(.17)	(.90)	(1.13)	(1.94)	(1.29)
HCHANG	-2.85	-.09	.13	.13	-.66	.37
	(.63)	(.19)	(.60)	(.45)	(.81)	(.56)
HENDUR	9.47a	-.66	.45	.01	-1.19	-.49
	(2.01)	(1.44)	(1.95)	(.03)	(1.40)	(.72)
HAGGRE	6.83	-.48	.41	.12	-1.25	-.01
	(1.43)	(1.04)	(1.76)	(.40)	(1.46)	(.01)
WDEFER	3.51	-.36	.14	.08	1.11	-.41
	(.70)	(.73)	(.55)	(.26)	(1.23)	(.57)
WORDER	-9.94a	.86	-.42	-.14	-1.47	1.07
	(2.05)	(1.82)	(1.74)	(.46)	(1.68)	(1.54)
WEXHIB	2.63	-.09	-.07	-.49	-1.63	-.84
	(.53)	(.20)	(.30)	(1.59)	(1.84)	(1.18)
WAUTON	-1.35	.00	-.06	.04	.14	-.80
	(.32)	(.00)	(.29)	(.14)	(.18)	(1.32)
WAFFIL	-6.39	.58	-.11	-.04	.94	.13
	(1.33)	(1.23)	(.47)	(.15)	(1.09)	(.18)
WINTRA	-3.06	.03	-.13	.04	-.81	-.02
	(.65)	(.08)	(.57)	(.14)	(.96)	(.02)
WSUCCR	3.93	-.29	-.05	-.47	.09	-.90
	(.79)	(.59)	(.19)	(1.52)	(.10)	(1.26)
WABASE	-1.80	.32	-.11	-.45	.65	.06
	(.41)	(.73)	(.51)	(1.61)	(.82)	(.09)
WNURTR	3.07	.12	-.14	.18	-1.34	.29
	(.61)	(.24)	(.55)	(.57)	(1.48)	(.41)
WCHANG	-2.74	.33	-.16	.11	.85	.11
	(.61)	(.76)	(.71)	(.41)	(1.05)	(.17)
WENDUR	5.43	-.24	.17	-.14	1.61	-.06
	(1.18)	(.53)	(.76)	(.50)	(1.94)	(.09)

Table A-3.2 (Continued)

	STLOY	STORE	SHILS	PUNID	SNDIS	|SNDIS|
WAGGRE	-5.03	.63	-.30	-.25	.52	.16
	(.93)	(1.20)	(1.12)	(.73)	(.53)	(.20)
WOMAGE	-1.81	.10	-.01	-.01	.53	-.14
	(.88)	(.50)	(.06)	(.04)	(1.45)	(.48)
FAMIZ	9.53	-.24	.54	-.07	-.03	2.54
	(.60)	(.16)	(.69)	(.07)	(.01)	(1.13)
OWNCAR	-1.49	-1.25	2.86	-2.98	28.57[a]	-11.75
	(.02)	(.20)	(.90)	(.74)	(2.47)	(1.27)
MKTSIZ	4.43[a]	.41[a]	-.22[a]	.54[a]	-.14	.21
	(3.37)	(3.19)	(3.32)	(6.59)	(.59)	(1.13)
INCOCC	-243.04	20.18	-9.78	7.27	-8.87	23.34
	(1.86)	(1.58)	(1.52)	(.89)	(.38)	(1.24)
T-total	1.75[a]	1.17	1.48	3.13[a]	1.58[a]	.81
F-ad	1.05	.63	.82	1.30	1.39	.71
R^2	.055	.038	.047	.095	.050	.026

*All coefficients transformed by Multiplying by 10^{-2}.
[a]Significant at the 5% level.

Table A−3.3

BEER VALIDATION SAMPLE REGRESSION COEFFICIENTS AND T-RATIOS FOR STORE BEHAVIOR VARIABLES*

(485 Households)

	STLOY	STORE	SHILS	SNDIS	|SNDIS|
HDEFER	8.07	-.79	.24	3.53	-2.52
	(1.57)	(1.16)	(.75)	(1.71)	(1.46)
HORDER	-7.43	.93	-.45	-.34	.79
	(1.54)	(1.45)	(1.50)	(.18)	(.49)
HEXHIB	4.95	-.06	.11	-4.75[a]	4.01[a]
	(.87)	(.08)	(1.33)	(2.08)	(2.10)
HAUTON	-1.49	-.24	-.02	1.38	.20
	(.32)	(.38)	(.08)	(.73)	(.12)
HAFFIL	-.59	-.32	-.09	-.21	-2.33
	(.10)	(.41)	(.24)	(.09)	(1.15)
HINTRA	-8.27	1.08	-.49	-.19	1.18
	(1.61)	(1.59)	(1.54)	(.09)	(.67)
HSUCCR	-1.55	.07	-.20	1.11	-1.67
	(.29)	(.10)	(.61)	(.52)	(.94)
HABASE	-.63	.17	-.02	-3.66	2.57
	(.12)	(.25)	(.06)	(1.74)	(1.46)
HNURTR	4.76	-.00	.30	.30	1.18
	(.82)	(.00)	(.85)	(.13)	(.61)
HCHANG	.42	.05	-.13	.47	.21
	(.08)	(.07)	(.41)	(.23)	(.12)
HENDUR	3.90	-.71	.14	-1.52	-.07
	(.74)	(1.02)	(.42)	(.72)	(.04)
HAGGRE	-4.48	.28	-.26	.80	-49.93[a]
	(.86)	(.41)	(.83)	(.39)	(2.03)
WDEFER	1.90	-.45	.10	-1.26	2.02
	(.33)	(.59)	(.27)	(.54)	(1.05)
WORDER	7.85	-.55	.42	.24	.64
	(1.49)	(.79)	(1.28)	(.11)	(.36)
WEXHIB	3.01	-.51	-.04	-1.56	-.08
	(.56)	(.71)	(.12)	(.72)	(.05)
WAUTON	1.05	-.38	.19	-1.13	.72
	(.22)	(.58)	(.64)	(.58)	(.44)
WAFFIL	-4.99	.56	-.21	-.81	1.40
	(.95)	(.80)	(.65)	(.38)	(.80)
WINTRA	-6.04	.98	-.29	-.16	1.27
	(1.22)	(1.50)	(.97)	(.08)	(.76)
WSUCCR	-5.68	.57	-.56	-3.08	2.73
	(1.11)	(.85)	(1.78)	(1.51)	(1.60)
WABASE	-2.80	.02	.02	-.01	-.39
	(.60)	(.03)	(.07)	(.01)	(.25)
WNURTR	4.64	-.18	.01	-1.82	.90
	(.85)	(.25)	(.04)	(.84)	(.49)

Table A-3.3 (Continued)

	STLOY	STORE	SHILS	SNDIS	|SNDIS|
WCHANG	-4.83	.73	-.29	.05	1.14
	(.98)	(1.11)	(.95)	(.03)	(.69)
WENDUR	-1.98	.20	-.30	-1.91	2.67
	(.42)	(.32)	(1.03)	(1.01)	(1.68)
WAGGRE	-9.86	1.17	-.72[a]	-3.12	3.35
	(1.70)	(1.53)	(2.04)	(1.34)	(1.73)
WOMAGE	.33	-.38	.06	-1.02	-.34
	(.14)	(1.19)	(.41)	(1.04)	(.41)
FAMSIZ	-.01	.41	-.40	3.93	-6.46
	(.00)	(.19)	(.40)	(.59)	(1.16)
OWNCAR	41.08	-5.65	4.53	39.25	-27.75
	(.48)	(.50)	(.86)	(1.11)	(.94)
MKTSIZ	.29	-.04	.07	-.10	.37
	(.19)	(.22)	(.78)	(.17)	(.74)
INCOCC	-350.12[a]	16.34	-15.74	53.96	-39.70
	(2.20)	(.78)	(1.61)	(.84)	(.74)
F-total	1.17	.87	.96	.86	.93
F-ad	1.04	.73	.52	.78	.97
R^2	.070	.052	.058	.052	.057

*All coefficients transformed by multiplying by 10^{-2}.
[a]Significant at the 5% level.

APPENDIX B

THE EDWARDS

PERSONAL PREFERENCE

SCHEDULE

This appendix presents a review of the recent literature pertaining to the technical adequacy, reliability, and validity of the Edwards Personal Preference Schedule as a measure of personality. It is presented in five sections: theory and description of the test, technical problems, reliability, validity, and factor-analysis studies. Reasonable effort was expended to examine all relevant literature through 1963, but no claim is made for exhaustiveness. Many studies were examined which may not be mentioned here because they are not directly pertinent, because another study covered the same area better, or in some cases, because of technical or methodological inadequacies.

THEORY AND DESCRIPTION OF TEST

The Edwards Personal Preference Schedule (EPPS) (see Edwards, 1959) is a paper-and-pencil, machine-scored test taking about 40-50 minutes to complete and consisting of 210 pairs of items. For each item, the subject is asked to indicate which member of the pair is most characteristic of himself. Since the members of each pair are roughly matched for "social desirability," the test is "forced-choice"; the subject presumably is forced to be honest, since both members of the pair are equally good (or bad).

146

The 210 pairs of statements are scaled on fifteen personality variables, of which each is paired twice with each of the other fourteen variables, plus a consistency scale that is made up of one repeated pair of statements for each of the fifteen variables. The fifteen personality variables are taken from a list of manifest needs presented by H.A. Murray (1938) and represent an extension of the biological or "derived-drive" theory of motivation that was current in the 1930's. Murray's definition of need is worth quoting in this context:

> "A need is a construct which stands for a force in the brain region, a force which organizes perception, apperception, intellection, conation, and action in such a way as to transform in a certain direction an existing unsatisfying situation. A need is sometimes provoked directly by internal processes of a certain kind, but more frequently (when in a state of readiness) by the occurrence of one of a few commonly effective press (environmental forces). Thus, it manifests itself by leading the organism to search for or to avoid encountering or, when encountered, to attend and respond to certain kinds of press. Each need is characteristically accompanied by a particular feeling or emotion and tends to use certain modes to further its trend. It may be weak or intense, momentary or enduring. But is usually persists and gives rise to a certain course of overt behavior (or fantasy) which changes the initiating circumstance in such a way as to bring about an end situation which stills (appeases or satisfies) the organism. (Murray, 1938, pp. 123-124.)

Murray distinguishes between primary needs, such as those for air, food, or water, and secondary (or psychogenic) needs, such as achievement, dominance, etc., which are presumably derived from the primary needs and have no focal or immediate connection with organic processes. All the needs measured by the EPPS are secondary. Murray's list has no claim to unique theoretical correctness: one man's list is empirically no better than another's. Making lists of needs is still popular, as shown by the list of "major social wants common to Western Man" given by Krech, Crutchfield, and Ballachey in their recent (1962) social psychology text: affiliation, acquisitiveness, prestige, power, altruism, and curiosity.

Murray's original (1938) list contained twenty needs, only twelve of which have names identical or similar to those used by Edwards. The eight need names not used by Edwards are: counteraction, defendance, harmavoidance, infavoidance, play, rejection, sentience, and understanding. Names used by Edwards but not by Murray are: intraception, change, and endurance. "Sentience" and "play" may have some relation to Edwards' "change" and "understanding" may have something to do with "intraception." "Endurance," as defined by Edwards, seems to have no counterpart in Murray's list of needs. Adding to the confusion over names, others have changed them further, presumably to make interpretation easier for lay audiences. For instance, in a report by the Advertising Research Foundation (1964), deference becomes "compliance," affiliation becomes "association," intraception becomes "analysis," succorance becomes "dependence," abasement becomes "self-depreciation," and nurturance becomes "assistance." Whether these names are better than Murray's is a matter of taste. Table B-1 gives Edwards' definitions of the variables and abbreviations for their names. Abbreviated definitions are given in Table 4-1 of Chapter 4.

The EPPS is an example of a "rational" approach to personality measurement in which preconceived categories, based on theory or hypotheses, are used as the basis for item construction and validation.

Table B-1

DEFINITIONS OF THE 15 SCALES OF THE EDWARDS PERSONAL REFERENCE PROFILE

1. Achievement: To do one's best, to be successful, to accomplish tasks requiring skill and effort, to be a recognized authority, to accomplish something of great significance, to do a difficult job well, to solve difficult problems and puzzles, to be able to do things better than others, to write a great novel or play.
2. Deference: To get suggestions from others, to find out what others think, to follow instructions and do what is expected, to praise others, to tell others that they have done a good job, to accept the leadership of others, to read about great men, to conform to custom and avoid the unconventional, to let others make decisions.
3. Order: To have written work neat and organized, to make plans before starting on a difficult task, to have things organized, to keep things neat and orderly, to make plans when taking a trip, to organize details of work, to keep letters and files according to some system, to have meals organized and a definite time for eating, to have things arranged so that they run smoothly without change.
4. Exhibition: To say witty and clever things, to tell amusing jokes and stories, to talk about personal adventures and experiences, to have others notice and comment upon one's appearance, to say things just to see what effect it will have on others, to talk about personal achievements, to be the center of attention, to use words that others do not know the meaning of, to ask questions others cannot answer.
5. Autonomy: To be able to come and go as desired, to say what one thinks about things, to be independent of others in making decisions, to feel free to do what one wants, to do things that are unconventional, to avoid situations where one is expected to conform, to do things without regard to what others may think, to criticize those in positions of authority, to avoid responsibilities and obligations.

6. Affiliation: To be loyal to friends, to participate in friendly groups, to do things for friends, to form new friendships, to make as many friends as possible, to share things with friends, to do things with friends rather than alone, to form strong attachments, to write letters to friends.

7. Intraception: To analyze one's motives and feelings, to observe others, to understand how others feel about problems, to put one's self in another's place, to judge people by why they do things rather than by what they do, to analyze the behavior of others, to analyze the motives of others, to predict how others will act.

8. Succorance: To have others provide help when in trouble, to seek encouragement from others, to have others be kindly, to have others be sympathetic and understanding about personal problems, to receive a great deal of affection from others, to have others do favors cheerfully, to be helped by others when depressed, to have others feel sorry when one is sick, to have a fuss made over one when hurt.

9. Dominance: To argue for one's point of view, to be a leader in groups to which one belongs, to be regarded by others as a leader, to be elected or appointed chairman of committees, to make group decisions, to settle arguments and disputes between others, to persuade and influence others to do what one wants, to supervise and direct the actions of others, to tell others how to do their jobs.

10. Abasement: To feel guilty when one does something wrong, to accept blame when things do not go right, to feel that personal pain and misery suffered does more good than harm, to feel the need for punishment for wrong doing, to feel better when giving in and avoiding a fight than when having one's own way, to feel the need for confession of errors, to feel depressed by inability to handle situations, to feel timid in the presence of superiors, to feel inferior to others in most respects.

11. Nurturance: To help friends when they are in trouble, to assist others less fortunate, to treat others with kindness and sympathy, to forgive others, to do small favors for others, to be generous with others, to sympathize with others who are hurt or sick, to show a great deal of affection toward others, to have others confide in one about personal problems.

12. Change: To do new and different things, to travel, to meet new people, to experience novelty and change in daily routine, to experiment and try new things, to eat in new and different places, to try new and different jobs, to move about the country and live in different places, to participate in new fads and fashions.

13.   Endurance: To keep at a job until it is finished, to complete any job undertaken, to work hard at a task, to keep at a puzzle or problem until it is solved, to work at a single job before taking on others, to stay up late working in order to get a job done, to put in long hours of work without distraction, to stick at a problem even though it may seem as if no progress is being made, to avoid being interrupted while at work.

14.   Heterosexuality: To go out with members of the opposite sex, to engage in social activities with the opposite sex, to be in love with someone of the opposite sex, to kiss those of the opposite sex, to be regarded as physically attractive by those of the opposite sex, to participate in discussions about sex, to read books and plays involving sex, to listen to or to tell jokes involving sex, to become sexually excited.

15.   Aggression: To attack contrary points of view, to tell others what one thinks about them, to criticize others publicly, to make fun of others, to tell others off when disagreeing with them, to get revenge for insults, to become angry, to blame others when things go wrong, to read newspaper accounts of violence.

It is also "ipsative" in the sense that the forced-choice format of the items allows determination only of the *relative* strength of the fifteen needs, and not of their absolute level. The main problem with the rational inventory is to establish the significance of the theoretical categories used through empirical validation research; some of this research on the EPPS is reported below

The two other currently popular paper-and-pencil personality instruments are the Minnesota Multiphasic Personality Inventory (MMPI) and the California Personality Inventory (CPI). Both are examples of the "empirical" approach to personality measurement in that the scales are constructed by determining which of a large number of items discriminate empirically between known groups (such as schizophrenics and normals, or people who make a good impression and those who do not). Both the MMPI and the CPI use a "yes-no" item format that can only be controlled for social desirability and faking by item wording and by building in lie scales. The problem with empirical scales is to explain *why* a group of items discriminates two given groups, a problem which is presumably dealt with in rationally developed scales by the theory on which they are based.

TECHNICAL PROBLEMS: TRANSPARENCY, FAKABILITY, AND SOCIAL DESIRABILITY

Because the responses required by the EPPS are subjective reports by the person taking the test, they are susceptible to various biases, conscious and unconscious. The subject may deliberately conceal or fake his reports about his preferences because he wishes to make a good impression, please the researcher, or avoid social sanctions. Even if the subject is trying to be completely honest in his reports, he may have needs of which he is completely unaware, or only vaguely aware. Obviously the EPPS cannot deal with unconscious motivation, since it relies solely on subjective reports. Some personality inventories are designed to deal with the "good impression" problem by making the items so subtle that the subject cannot see through them. Edwards made no effort to deal with this "transparency problem" in constructing the scale, and it turns out to be rather transparent. Korman and Coltharp (1962) gave definitions of the fifteen scales of the EPPS to subjects and asked them to guess which items went with which scales; they did so with 77 percent accuracy. Mann (1958) had subjects fill out self-ratings on each of the fifteen needs; ten of them correlated at the .05 level with EPPS scores on the same needs.

If a test is transparent, it can usually also be faked (i.e., the subject can make himself "look good" on the test). Edwards attempted to deal with this problem by using the forced-choice format in which the subject is asked to choose one of two equally "good"-looking state-ments as more characteristic of himself. The trick lies in getting pairs of statements with identical "social desirability" values, these values being the same for all subjects taking the test. Another way of dealing with the faking issue, also used by Edwards, is to build in repeated pairs of items and check the consistency with which subjects respond. Borislow (1958) showed that neither of these efforts was completely successful with the EPPS. He gave the test twice to three groups of subjects. On the second administration, one group was told to give responses which would be considered "socially desirable" (SD), another was told to give responses they considered "personally desirable" (PD), and a third (control) was told to give a self-appraisal, as were all groups on the first administration. Compared to the control group, both SD and PD groups had lower self-profile correlations between the first and second administrations, and consistency scores (a kind of faking key) were lower only in the SD condition; in other words, responses were differ-ent, and faking was not detected by the consistency key under the PD instructions (the PD instructions essentially followed Whyte's (1956) advice on how to take personality tests). It must be concluded that the EPPS is fakable and that the consistency scale may or may not identify the faker.

One possible reason for the transparency and fakability of the EPPS was uncovered by Corah, et al (1958). Using thirty item pairs (two from each of the fifteen scales) from the EPPS, subjects were asked to pick the more socially desirable member. They were able to do so eas-ily and with good agreement. Later, other subjects were asked to fill out the thirty items as a self-description, and the percent choosing the (previously determined) more desirable member of each pair was plotted against item desirability. Product-moment *r* was .88, accounting for 77 percent of the variance. Thus, it appears that item pairs are not perfectly matched for social desirability in the EPPS, and that social desirability alone accounts for some of the variation in scores.

Further evidence on this point is contributed by Saltz, Reece, and Ager (1962). They administered the EPPS under instructions to give socially desirable responses on all items. They found large and consistent *individual* differences in the social desirability of the scale items, but conclude that Edwards was able largely to eliminate the effect of group differences in social desirability because there was little agreement among subjects as to which items were more desirable (a result which conflicts with the findings of Corah, et al, above). Some writers have argued that individual differences in perception of item desirability are correlated with possession of the need being measured and therefore can be ignored; Saltz, et al, point out that this argument may hold for generally desirable traits, but some traits are repressed or denied and therefore would not appear on this kind of test. They did find that individual differences in social desirability varied for each scale, a hopeful sign for the EPPS.

Finally, Edwards himself (Edwards, 1957) did extensive research on the relation of social desirability to item choice. He scaled all items in the EPPS separately on a scale of social desirability (SD) and correlated the difference between members of the same item pair on the SD scale with the probability of endorsement of the higher item. The product-moment *r* was .40, indicating that 16 percent of the variance in item choice on the EPPS can be accounted for by the SD variable. He also quotes Wright as having found a similar correlation of .45, and Klett, .37. If the same items are administered in a yes-no format (like the MMPI and the CPI, among others) instead of the forced-choice, the correlation between SD and item choice jumps to .87, accounting for 76 percent of the variance. Edwards concluded that the forced-choice format was largely successful in minimizing the influence of social desirability in item choice.

In summary, it is fair to say that the EPPS is handicapped by not being able to measure unconscious motivation and by having been proved to be transparent and fakable, and by the proven connection between social desirability of an item and the probability of its being endorsed. Researchers using it must be willing to rely on the good will of their subjects not to fake it consciously and to try to answer it as honestly as possible, and they have no hope of measuring unconscious needs. Balanced against these disadvantages is its relatively nonthreatening character, ease of administration and interpretation, and the large volume of validation research which now supports it.

RELIABILITY

Reliability is the extent to which a measuring instrument gives the same result when applied repeatedly. If an instrument gives entirely different results each time it is applied, it is either not reliable or whatever it measures is changing rapidly. There are two generally accepted ways of determining reliability of a test: the split-half method, in which two halves of a test are correlated (with a correction for shortening of the test), and the repeated-measurements (stability) method, in which the whole test is administered twice and the results correlated. Table B-2 gives split-half and stability coefficients for each of the 15 scales.

Table B-2 shows the EPPS to have very satisfactory reliability. Comparatively speaking, intelligence tests usually have reliabilities in the .90's and attitude scales show reliability in the .60-.80 range. Most of the EPPS reliabilities are in the .70's and .80's, which is certainly adequate to use the scale scores for predicting other variables. Whatever the test measures reliably enough for group predictions, but probably not reliably enough for individual counseling.

Table B-2
RELIABILITY COEFFICIENTS FOR
THE 15 EPPS VARIABLES[a]

Variable	Split-half*	Stability**
1. Achievement	.74	.74
2. Deference	.60	.78
3. Order	.74	.87
4. Exhibition	.61	.74
5. Autonomy	.76	.83
6. Affiliation	.70	.77
7. Intraception	.79	.86
8. Succorance	.76	.78
9. Dominance	.81	.87
10. Abasement	.84	.88
11. Nurturance	.78	.79
12. Change	.79	.83
13. Endurance	.81	.86
14. Heterosexuality	.87	.85
15. Aggression	.84	.78

[a]From Edwards, 1959.
*Based on a national sample of 1509 college students.
**Based on 89 college students who took the test twice at one-week intervals.

VALIDITY

Validity is the degree to which an instrument measures what it is supposed to measure. There are two main ways of establishing the validity of a psychological measure: by relating it to another, purportedly similar measure (concurrent validity), and by relating it to behavior which the measure can reasonably be supposed to predict or imply (construct validity). Validity of each of the scales, as reported in the literature, will be discussed in turn.

1. *Achievement scale.* The need for achievement has usually been measured by the Thematic Apperception Test (TAT), a projective device developed by Murray. Naturally, for concurrent validity it should correlate with the EPPS achievement scale, but it failed to do so in two studies. Bendig (1957) correlated the EPPS achievement scale with the TAT measure of n achievement and with Taylor's Manifest Anxiety Scale. Based on data from 244 college sophomores, the correlation between the TAT measure and the EPPS measure was .11, not significant. Bendig concluded that either the two scales measure different things or that the TAT measure's lack of stability accentuated the relation. Melikian (1957) administered the same two measures to eighty-four Arabic-speaking students at the American University in Beirut and found a correlation of .16, also not significant. It seems reasonable to conclude that the subjective and projective measures of the need for achievement do not give the same results.

The EPPS achievement scale was found to correlate negatively (-.22) with need for security (measured by a separate scale) by Blum (1961). Dunnette, et al (1958) correlated scores on the EPPS with scores on the California Personality Inventory. In a sample of 102 young white-collar men, they found that the EPPS achievement scale correlated with the CPI scales for dominance, responsibility, socialization, and good impression. Perhaps more significantly, it failed to correlate with CPI scales for achievement via conformity, or achievement via independence. Allen (1957) correlated the EPPS and the MMPI scales, using a sample of 130 college sophomores. For males only, the EPPS achievement scale correlated only with the MMPI validity scale, which measures "rational" responses to the MMPI items.

Testing construct validity, Shaw (1961) found that the EPPS achievement score failed to differentiate between academic over-and under-achievers, but so did the TAT *n* achievement score. Kazmier (1961) found no relation between EPPS scores and success in a psychology course, but this is not terribly damaging evidence given the nature of these grades as a criterion. Worell (1960) found that subjects high on the EPPS achievement scale were superior to low scorers on two difficult verbal-learning tasks. Garrison and Scott (1962) found that subjects high on the EPPS achievement scale were superior to low scorers on two difficult verbal-learning tasks. Garrison and Scott (1962) found that EPPS achievement scores among education students were correlated with marital status (married were higher), and with academic average. Quoting from the brief review of the EPPS by Katzell & Katzell (1962), "Weiss, Wertheimer, and Groesbeck (1959) found a correlation of .42 between the EPPS achievement score and academic average . . . . Demos and Spolyar (1961) found no differences between the average EPPS scores of college students whose academic perform- ance was in line with their aptitude and those of overachieving and underachieving college students. However, Krug (1959) found that overachievers scored significantly higher than underachievers on the achievement, endurance, and other scales, and lower on the affiliation and heterosexuality scales."

The evidence on the validity of EPPS achievement scale is mixed. It has low concurrent validity and only fair construct validity. It fails to correlate with the TAT and CPI measures of achievement motivation; about half the studies reviewed found some relation between scores on the achievement scale and relevant behaviors.

2. *Deference scale.* Dunnette, et al found significant relations between the EPPS deference scale and CPI scales for responsibility, self-control, and good impression. Allen found a correlation for females of -.37 between deference and the F (schizophrenia) scale of the MMPI, which he interprets as an inability of schizophrenics to be dependent on others. Levy (1962) found that deference scores were correlated -.22 with positive expectations for change, and Blum (1961) found deference associated (.17) with desire for security.

Using the Asch situation to create pressures toward conformity, Appley and Moeller (1963) found that deference scores were *not* corre- lated with conformity scores, as did Bernardin and Jessor (1957) and Gisvold (1958). But Bernardin and Jessor constructed an index of "de- pendency" (above 70 percent on deference and below 50 percent on autonomy) and found that "dependent" subjects performed badly on a punishing task and requested help more often on a difficult task. Izard (1960) constructed an experimental situation in which social pressure was applied to subjects, and did *not* find deference to be correlated with resistance to social pressures. Garrison and Scott (1962) found their married education students higher on deference than those single, and graduate students higher than undergraduates. Zuckermann (1958) found that student nurses rated as "rebellious" by peers were signifi- cantly lower on the deference scale. Summarizing, the evidence on the deference scale is fairly thin; concurrent validity is reasonable, although the correlations are low, and construct validity remains shaky, failing on four out of six efforts to validate.

3. *Order scale.* Dunnette, et al found the EPPS order scale corre- lated negatively with CPI scales for dominance, capacity for status,

sociability, social presence, tolerance, communality, achievement via independence, intellectual efficiency, psychological-mindedness, and flexibility. It was correlated positively with the CPI femininity scale. Allen (1957) found the order scale strongly positively correlated for females with the MMPI lie scale and with suppression, suggesting that orderly people lie about or to themselves defensively. Blum (1961) found the order scale positively related to need for security.

Lubin, Levitt, and Zuckermann (1962) found that student nurses who returned a voluntary questionnaire were higher on order than those who did not. Garrison and Scott found married students higher on order, as were students with high academic averages.

In summary, the order scale appears to have very good concurrent validity, especially in terms of its correlations with the CPI, and reasonably good construct validity, although there is not much evidence on the latter.

4. *Exhibition scale.* EPPS exhibition scores were found to be positively correlated with CPI scales for dominance, capacity for status, sociability, social presence, self-acceptance, and intellectual efficiency by Dunnette, et al. Allen found the exhibition scale had a strong negative correlation with social introversion on the MMPI.

No evidence on the construct validity of the exhibition scale could be found in literature.

Concurrent validity seems reasonably good, but the relation between behavior and the exhibition scale remains to be determined.

5. *Autonomy scale.* Dunnette, et al found no correlation between the autonomy scale and the 18 CPI scales. Allen found autonomy correlated for males with the MMPI validity scale and for his total group, suggesting that highly autonomous people respond more "rationally" to taking the MMPI. He also found for females that the autonomy scale correlated positively with the psychopathic deviate scale and with the total group, suggesting that autonomous people have less regard or consideration for others. Blum found autonomy negatively correlated with desire for security. Zuckermann and Goode (1958) found that the Sway test, which predicts hypnotizability, was negatively related to autonomy scores in a sample of twenty-seven student nurses. Gynther, Miller, and Davis (1962) found among ninety-five subjects that the autonomy scale correlated with three of the four scales on Leary's Interpersonal Check List: positively with competitiveness, and negatively with responsibility and love.

Four investigators have used the Asch conformity situation (in which a subject is confronted with unanimous wrong judgments in a group and asked to give his own judgment) to test the validity of the autonomy scale. Appley and Moeller (1963), Bernardin and Jessor (1957), and Lipetz and Milton (1962) all failed to fill any relationship between conformity and autonomy. Gisvold, using thirty-one males and nineteen females from a psychology course, found a correlation of -.54 between conformity and the EPPS autonomy score. As quoted above, Bernardine and Jessor constructed a "dependency" index, choosing subjects above 70 percent on deference and below 50 percent on autonomy, and found that these subjects performed badly on a task under punishing conditions and asked for help and confirmation more frequently. Jessor (1963) criticizes the Lipetz and Milton study because they used only part of the total EPPS, and because their experimental situation was different from his. Izard's (1960) study of resistance to interpersonal influence yielded a correlation of .38 between the EPPS autonomy scale and that measure. Zuckermann (1958) found that student nurses rated as "rebellious" by their peers scored significantly higher on autonomy than those rated submissive.

Summarizing, it seems fair to conclude that the autonomy scale has good concurrent validity and fairly good construct validity. One could wish it had higher correlations with some of the CPI measures and that the relation of autonomy to conformity were a little more clear.

6. *Affiliation scale.* In their research, Dunnette, et al found the affiliation scale to be correlated only with the tolerance and good impression scales of the CPI. Allen found affiliation weakly (.23) related to the validity scale of the MMPI, a result that is hard to interpret. Gynther, Miller, and Davis report that affiliation scores are negatively related to competitiveness and positively related to love on the Leary Interpersonal Check List.

No studies of the construct validity of the affiliation scale were found in the literature.

This scale, therefore, remains only weakly validated.

7. *Intraception scale.* The intraception scale, a measure of the need to understand personal motivations, correlated with eight of the CPI scales in the study by Dunnette, et al. Positive correlations were obtained with capacity for status, sociability, well-being, responsibility, self-control, tolerance, good impression, and achievement via conformity. Tolor (1961) found a correlation of .31 between the intraception scale and the Insight Test among sixty-seven psychiatric aides. Levy found that expectancy for change correlated positively with intraception.

No studies were found bearing on the construct validity of the intraception scale.

Thus, while this scale has good concurrent validity, its relation to behavior remains to be determined.

8. *Succorance scale.* Dunnette, et al found seven significant relationships, all negative, between the succorance scale, which measures the need to be helped, and the CPI variables of dominance, capacity for status, well-being, responsibility, tolerance, good impression, and

achievement via conformity. Allen found no correlations between succorance and the MMPI scales. In other tests of concurrent validity: Gynther, Miller, and Davis found significant negative correlations between succorance and the Leary Interpersonal Check List scales for competitiveness and dominance, and Blum found that need for security was positively correlated with succorance.

Garrison and Scott found married students significantly lower on succorance than the unmarried, and that students planning a long career in teaching were lower than those planning to teach only for a short time. Zuckermann's (1962) rebellious nurses were lower on succorance than submissive ones.

Thus, the concurrent validity on the succorance scale of the EPPS is good (except for its failure to correlate with the MMPI), but its construct validity can only be called fair because of the low volume of evidence on the latter.

9. *Dominance scale.* Nine of the CPI scales correlate significantly (all positively) with the EPPS dominance scale among the young male white-collar workers in the sample of Dunnette, et al. They are: dominance, capacity for status, sociability, self-acceptance, responsibility, tolerance, good impression, achievement via conformity, and intellectual efficiency. Allen found a negative correlation between dominance and the MMPI scale for social introversion. Levy found that dominance correlated negatively with expectation for change, a result that is difficult to assess, and Blum found dominance negatively related to need for security. Gynther, Miller and Davis found EPPS dominance to be positively correlated with the scales for competitiveness and dominance on the Leary Interpersonal Check List.

Mogar (1962) found that females who showed improvement under competition on a block design test score higher on the EPPS dominance scale than those who did not. Zuckermann's rebellious student nurses were higher on dominance than others. Izard (1960) found that dominance scores on the EPPS were correlated with a measure of resistance to interpersonal influence. Garrison and Scott showed that dominance scores were correlated with the number of years that education students plan to teach.

In summary, the EPPS dominance scale seems well-validated, in both concurrent and construct validity studies.

10. *Abasement scale.* Among Dunnette's white-collar males, the EPPS abasement scale is negatively correlated with dominance, capacity for status, sociability, socialization, tolerance, and achievement via conformity on the CPI. Allen found abasement correlated positively with social introversion on the MMPI. Gynther, Miller, and Davis found that the abasement scale was correlated negatively with competitiveness and positively with love on the Leary Interpersonal Check List. Blum (1961) found abasement correlated positively with need for security.

Zuckermann's rebellious student nurses were lower than others on abasement, and Izard found abasement negatively correlated with resistance to interpersonal influence. Appley and Moeller found impressive evidence for the validity of the abasement scale: using the Asch situation to measure conformity in forty-one freshmen women and correlating these scores with personality measures from the CPI, Gordon Personal Profile, and the EPPS, the only significant correlation between conformity and other personality scales (out of at least 12 possible) was with the EPPS abasement scale. Garrison and Scott found sophomores higher on abasement than juniors, and juniors higher than graduate students.

The abasement scale seems to be well validated.

11. *Nurturance scale.* Nurturance, or the need to help others, was correlated with only three of the CPI scales in Dunnette's sample: negatively with self-acceptance, and positively with well-being and self-control. Allen found a strong negative correlation between nurturance and the psychopathic deviate scale on the MMPI and interprets this as meaning that nurturant people have a high regard for other. Gynther, Miller, and Davis report that nurturance is negatively correlated with competitiveness and positively with love on the Leary Check List, as was the abasement scale.

Garrison and Scott found that those education students who went to college to learn to teach had higher nurturance scores than those who went to be informed, and that sophomores had higher nurturance scores than seniors and graduate students.

It appears that the concurrent validity of the nurturance scale is good, but that evidence on its construct validity is meager.

12. *Change scale.* Dunnette, et al found only social presence on the CPI significantly correlated with the EPPS change scale. Allen found no relationships between the change scale and the MMPI. Legy's expectation-for-change scale correlated positively, but not highly (.29) with the EPPS change measure. Blum found a correlation of -.34 between need for security and change.

Seniors and graduate students are higher on the change scale than juniors, who are higher than sophomores, according to Garrison and Scott. No other evidence on the construct validity of the change scale could be found.

Thus, the change scale shows reasonable (but not impressive) concurrent validity, and there is too little evidence on its construct validity to make a judgment.

13. *Endurance scale.* Endurance correlated positively with five of the CPI scales in Dunnette's sample: well-being, responsibility, self-control, good impression, and achievement via conformity; and negatively with two: self-acceptance and communality. Allen found a negative correlation between endurance and psychasthenia which he inter-

preted as meaning that high-endurance people do *not* deal compulsively with threat.

Garrison and Scott found that married education students were higher on endurance than single ones, and that those who planned long teaching careers were higher than those who intended to teach only a short time (very pleasing evidence for the endurance scale); he also found a very strong relation between academic average and endurance.

It can be concluded that the concurrent validity of the endurance scale is good, and that the data on construct validity, although based on only one study, is fairly convincing.

14. *Heterosexuality scale.* The heterosexuality scale of the EPPS is *negatively* correlated with five of the CPI scales in Dunnette's sample of white-collar males: well-being, responsibility, socialization, good impression, and achievement via conformity. The correlation with good impression is especially strong (-.38), suggesting that people with strong heterosexual needs do not impress others favorably. Allen found a positive correlation among female students between heterosexuality and the MMPI scale for schizophrenia, suggesting that girls with strong heterosexual needs are not reality-oriented. It seems worth noting, at this point, that heterosexuality is *not* significantly correlated with love on the Leary Interpersonal Check List.

Garrison and Scott found that married students express lower heterosexual needs than single students, and that students who do *not* plan a long teaching career have higher heterosexual needs than those who do; juniors have higher heterosexuality scores than either sophomores or seniors and graduate students. Gynther, Miller, and Davis (1962) report a correlation between EPPS heterosexuality and an index of "positive relations with men" among forty-two student nurses, i.e., those who were engaged or married or who dated frequently.

To summarize, the heterosexuality scale has adequate concurrent validity, the pattern of its correlations with other instruments suggesting that high heterosexuality scores indicate relatively poor adjustment. The construct validity studies show reasonable correlations with other indicators of heterosexual needs.

15. *Aggression scale.* In Dunnette's study, five of the CPI scales (on which "good" is always a high score) correlate negatively with the EPPS aggression scale: well-being, responsibility, self-control, tolerance, and good impression. Aggression was not related to MMPI scales in Allen's sample. Responsibility and love on the Leary Interpersonal Check List are negatively related to EPPS aggression scores, and competitiveness is positively related to aggression.

Lubin, Levitt, and Zuckermann (1962) found that student nurses who returned a voluntary questionnaire were lower on aggression than those who did not, and Zuckermann's rebellious nurses were higher on aggression than others. Garrison and Scott found that education students with low academic averages were higher on aggression than those with high averages.

Although the amount of evidence on the validity of the aggression scale is not great, what there is indicates adequate and reasonable validity correlations.

SUMMARY.

In summarizing all the validity studies reported above, it is clear that the EPPS shows good concurrent validity. Enough research has been done to allow judgments on the concurrent validity of all fifteen scales. Of these, only the achievement scale has poor concurrent validity, largely because of its failure to correlate with Murray's projective measure. Three scales—deference, affiliation, and change—can be said to have only fair concurrent validity; all the rest have either good or very good correlations with other measures of the same variables.

The evidence on the construct validity of the EPPS is less clear. There was too little evidence in the literature to permit making a judgment on the construct validity of four of the scales: exhibition, affiliation, intraception, and change. On the deference scale, construct validity can only be called fair because of its failure to correlate with conformity behavior. The pattern of results here suggests that perhaps deference is more related to the way subjects relate to superiors, rather than to peers, but this interpretation is definitely not suggested by the description of the scale. (See Table A-1.) The achievement scale shows mixed results on construct validity: some investigators found it related to actual achievement and some did not. There is too little evidence on the construct validity of the succorance scale for it to be considered good, but the little evidence seems to be in the right direction. All the rest of the scales (order, autonomy, dominance, abasement, nurturance, endurance, heterosexuality, and aggression) have good construct validity, having been shown to correlate fairly well with other measures or indicators of the same needs.

A final question on the validity of the EPPS—how much of the variance in behavior can one reasonably expect to account for with "personality" as measured by the Edwards test? It is a truism in social science that behavior is multi-determined: any given whole behavior act may have hundreds of determinants in the immediate situation surrounding the act, in the learning and past experience of the individual, as well as in that "relatively enduring set of predispositions to respond in systematic ways to given classes of stimuli" that is called "personality." A rough guess as to the maximum predictive power one can expect from personality scores can be based on the literature reviewed above. Not all the investigators gave data that would allow such an estimate, but Gisvold (1958) found a correlation of -.54 between the autonomy scale and conformity behavior in the Asch situation, accounting for 29 percent of the variance. Izard (1960) found three of the scales correlated with resistance to interpersonal influence: autonomy, .38; dominance, .38; and abasement, -.35; accounting for 14, 14, and 11 percents of the variance, respectively. Given the low intercorrelations among the scales, one might reasonably expect maximum multiple correlations between .50 and .60 for these data, accounting for perhaps 25-35 per cent of the variance in reliably measured criterion behavior. Generally speaking, slightly better correlations are possible in predicting achievement from intellectual tests: multiple R's of .65 are not too uncommon. This represents the most optimistic prediction; the average multiple R's will no doubt be lower than these.

FACTOR-ANALYSIS STUDIES OF THE EPPS

Not many factor analyses of the EPPS have been carried out, perhaps because of the low intercorrelations among the scales. In the most extensive work to date, Levonian, et al (1959) factor-analyzed the items in each of the fifteen scales separately, expecting to find a general factor in each corresponding to the need measured. Using phi-coefficients, they found the average inter-item correlation very low (.08), which precluded the discovery of a G factor; the factors they identified were based on the accidents of item pairing, rather than on any clearly identifiable item content. The authors attribute these results to Edwards' use of the forced-choice format, to his use of the same statement in different item-pairs and to the scoring of the same item in different scales. This study casts some doubt on the reality of the names given by Edwards to the scales, but a more appropriate test of this question would have been to factor all 210 items together, a job which has not yet been done. Low inter-item correlations within scales are no flaw in scale construction, since one presumably can get higher item validity this way.

Hartley and Allen (1959) factored the scale scores from the EPPS and the MMPI together, extracting ten factors by the centroid method and rotating graphically to oblique simple structure. Two of the factors had highest loadings on the EPPS scales, two in the MMPI, and six were mixtures of both. One EPPS factor has positive loadings on deference, order, and endurance, and negative loadings on autonomy and change. The other EPPS factor has positive high loadings on succorance and affiliation, and negative ones on intraception and autonomy. Another primarily EPPS factor has positive loadings for nurturance and abasement, negative loadings for aggression, exhibition, and achievement on the EPPS, and negative loadings for psychopathic deviance on the MMPI. The "sick" factors from the MMPI tended not to have loadings on the EPPS scales, indicating that they measure different things.

Finally, Heilizer (1963) did a Q-technique factor analysis of eighty people's scores on the EPPS. This involved obtaining the correlations of each person with every other person over the fifteen scale scores, and factoring the resulting "people matrix." Four different groups of people were in the sample: twenty college students, twenty neurotics, twenty people with personality disorders, and twenty schizophrenics. The first 8 factors accounts for 82 percent of the common variance, and the average communality was .49, considerably higher than would be possible with ordinary r-technique correlations of the EPPS. Factors were rotated analytically by the varimax method. Factor 1 contained mostly people with personality disorders, some neurotics, and some schizophrenics. They had higher scores than the sample average on the EPPS scales for endurance, abasement, nurturance and order, which the author interprets as their denial of their real needs. Factor 2 people (mostly students) were high on heterosexuality, endurance, and dominance, and low on succorance, nurturance, abasement, and aggression. The author interpreted this as a "strength" factor. The other factors are difficult to interpret, since they contain rather few people, a difficulty common with ipsative factor analysis.

The factoral studies do not shed much light on the factorial structure of the EPPS, except to say that it does not apparently measure the "sicker" aspects of personality picked up by the MMPI, and that sicker people may get elevated scores on the EPPS variables on which an outsider would rate them as low. It is clear from the intercorrelations among the scales that a factor analysis would have relatively limited usefulness for factor scores, since the common variance among the scales is low.

CONCLUSIONS

1. Technically, the EPPS seems to have adequate, but not perfect, controls for faking and social desirability, and little control for transparency. Also, it cannot measure unconscious needs.

2. It has adequate reliability for prediction on a group basis, but probably not for individual counseling.

3. The concurrent and construct validity of most of the scales is such as to justify using the EPPS to measure the needs it purports to measure. The achievement scale is the only one with poor enough results to make it of doubtful validity.

4. Factor-analytic studies thus far have not conclusively established its underlying structure.

REFERENCES

Advertising Research Foundation. *Are Threre Consumer Types?* New York: Advertising Research Foundation, 3 East 54th Street, 1964.

Allen, R.M. The relationship between the Edwards Personal Preference Schedule and the MMPI scales. *Journal of Applied Psychology*, 1957, *41*.

Anderson, T.W. *Introduction to Multivariate Statistical Analysis.* New York: John Wiley & Sons, Inc., 1958.

Anderson, T.W. and L.A. Goodman. Statistical inference about Markov chains, *Annals of Math. Stat.*, 1957, *28*, 89-110.

Appley, M. and G. Moeller. Conforming behavior and personality variables in college women. *J. Abnorm. Soc. Psychol.*, 1963, *66*, 284-290.

Bendig, A.W. Manifest anxiety and projective and objective measures of need achievement. *J. Consult. Psychol.*, 1957, *21*, 354.

Bernardin, A.C. and R. Jessor. A construct validation of the Edwards Personal Preference Schedule with respect to dependency. *J. Consult. Psychol.*, 1957, *21*, 63-67.

Blum, S.H. The desire for security. *J. Educ. Psychol.*, 1961, *52*, 317-321.

Borislow, B. The Edwards Personal Preference Schedule (EPPS) and fakability. *J. Appl. Psychol.*, 1958, *42*, 22-27.

Boyd, H.W., Jr. and R. Westfall. *An Evaluation of Continuous Consumer Panels as a Source of Marketing Information.* Chicago: American Marketing Association, 1960.

Brown, G., Brand Loyalty—fact or fiction? *Adv. Age*, XXIII (June 19, 1962), 53-55; (June 30, 1952), 45-47; (July 14, 1952), 54-56; (July 28, 1952), 46-48; (August 11, 1952), 56-58; (September 1, 1952), 80-82; (October 6, 1952) 82-86; (December 1, 1952), 76-79; XXIV (January 26, 1953), 75-76.

Bush, R.R. and F. Mosteller. *Stochastic Models for Learning.* New York: John Wiley & Sons, Inc., 1955.

Claycamp, H.J., and W.F. Massy. A new approach to market segmentation. Working paper No. 104, Graduate School of Business, Stanford University, June, 1966.

Cooley, W.J. and P.R. Lohnes. *Multrivariate Procedure for the Behavioral Sciences.* New York: John Wiley, 1962.

Corah, M.L. et al. Social desirability as a variable in the Edwards Personal Preference Schedule. *J. Consult. Psychol.*, 1958, *22*, 70-72.

Cunningham, R. Customer loyalty to store and brand. *Harvard Bus. Rev.*, 1961, *39*, 127-137.

—— Measurement of brand loyalty. *The Marketing Revolution.* New York: American Marketing Association, 1955.

Dixon, W. J. *BMD: Biomedical Computer Programs.* University of California, Los Angeles, January, 1964.

Duhamel, W.F.. The use of variable Markov processes as a partial basis for the determination and analysis of market segments. Unpublished PhD. Dissertation, Stanford University, 1966.

Dunnette, M., W. Kirchner and J. DeGidio. Relations among scores on Edwards Personal Preference Schedule, California Personal Inventory and Strong Vocational Interest Blank for an industrial sample. *J. Appl. Psychol.*, 1958, *42*, 178-181.

Edwards, A.L. *Manual for the Edwards Personal Preference Schedule.* New York: The Psychological Corporation, 1959.

—— *The Social Desirability Variable in Personality Assessment and Research.* New York: The Dryden Press, 1957.

Ehrenberg, A.S.C. The pattern of consumer. purchases. *Appl. Stat.*, 1959, *8*, 26-41.

Evans, F.B. Psychological and objective factors in the prediction of brand choice. *J. of Bus.*, 1959, *32*, 340-369.

Frank, R.E. Brand choice as a probability process, *J. Bus.*, 1962, *35*, 43-56.

—— The prediction of brand choice using simple probability models. Unpublished Ph.D. dissertation at the University of Chicago, 1960.

Frank, R.E. and H.W. Boyd. Are private-brand-prone grocery customers really different? *J. Adv. Res.*, 1965, *5*, 27-35.

Frank, R.E., S.P. Douglas and R.E. Polli. Household correlates of "brand loyalty" for grocery products. University of Pennsylvania, Mimeo., February, 1967.

Frank, R.E., A.A. Kuehn and W.F. Massy. *Quantitative Techniques in Marketing Analysis.* Homewood, Ill: Irwin, 1962.

Frank, R.E. and W.F. Massy. Estimating the effects of short-term promotional strategy in selected market segments. In Patrick Robinson and Charles Hinkle (eds.) *Sales Promotion Analysis: Some Applications of Quantitative Techniques.* Boston: Allyn and Bacon, forthcoming, 1968.

—— Market segmentation and the effectiveness of a brand's price and dealing policies. *J. Bus.*, 1965, *38*, 186-200.

Frank, R.E., W.F. Massy and H.W. Boyd, Jr. Correlates of grocery product consumption. *J. Mktg. Res.*, 1967, *4*.

Garrison, K. and M.H. Scott. Relationship of selected personal characteristics to the needs of college students preparing to teach. *Educ. Psychol. Measmt.*, 1962, *22*, 753-758.

Gisvold, D. A validity study of the autonomy and deference subscales of the Edwards Personal Preference Schedule, *J. Consult. Psychol.*, 1958, *22*, 445-447.

Gottlieb, M.J., Segmentation by personality types. From L. Stockman (ed.) *Advancing Marketing Efficiency.* Chicago: American Marketing Association, 1958, 148-58.

Gray Advertising Agency. Herd hysteria: a mounting marketing hazard. *Gray Matter,* 1965, *36.*

Gynther, M., F.T, Miller and H. Davis. Relations between needs and behavior as measured by the Edwards Personal Preference Schedule and Interpersonal Check List. *J. Social Psychol.*, 1962, *57*, 445-451.

Harman, H.H. *Modern Factor Analysis.* Chicago: University of Chicago, 1960.

Hartley, R. and R.M. Allén. The MMPI and the Edwards Personal Preference Schedule: a factor-analytic study. *J. Social Psychol.*

Heilizer, Fred. An ipsative factor analysis of the ipsative EPPS. *Psychol. Rep.,* 1963, *12,* 285-286.

Howard, R.A. Dynamic inference. *Op. Res.,* 1965, *13,* 712-733.

Industrial Surveys Company (Market Research Corporation of America). *Problems of Establishing a Consumer Panel in the New York Metropolitan Area.* Washington: U.S. Govt. Printing Office, 1952.

Izard, C. Personality characteristics associated with resistance to change. *J. Consult. Psychol.,* 1960, *24,* 437-440.

Jessor, R. On studying autonomy — without deference. *Psychol. Rep.,* 1963, *12,* 132-134.

Katzell, R. and M. Katzell. Development and application of structured tests of personality. *Rev. Educ. Res.,* 1962, *32,* 51-63.

Kazmier, L.V. Cross-validation groups, extreme groups, and the prediction of academic achievement, *J. Educ. Psychol.,* 1961, *52,* 195-198.

Koponen, A. Personality characteristics of purchasers, *J. Adv. Res.,* 1960, *1,* 6-12.

———— The influence of demographic factors on responses to the Edwards Personal Preference Schedule. Unpublished Ph.D. dissertation, Columbia University, 1957.

Korman, M. and F. Coltharp. Transparence in the EPPS. *J. Consult. Psychol.,* 1962, *26,* 379-382.

Krech, D., R. Crutchfield and E. Ballachey. *Individual in Society.* New York: McGraw-Hill, 1962.

Kuehn, A.A. An analysis of the dynamics of consumer behavior and its implications for marketing management. Unpublished Ph. D. dissertation, Carnegie Institute of Technology, 1958.

————Consumer Brand choice—a learning process? *J. Adv. Res.,* 1962, *2.*

Levonian, E. et al. A statistical evaluation of the Edwards Personal Preference Profile, *J. Appl. Psychol.*, 1959, *43*, 355-359.

Levy, L.H. Age and personal need correlates of expectancy for change. *Percept. Mot. Skills*, 1962, *15*, 351-356.

Lipetz, M. and G. Milton. Prediction of autonomy behavior from situational modifications of the EPPS in autonomy scales. *Psychol. Rep.*, 1962, *11*, 487-493.

Lipstein, B., The dynamics of brand loyalty and brand switching. *Better Measurements of Advertising Effectiveness: The Challenge of the 1960's.* Proceedings: 5th Annual Conference of the Adv. Res. Found. New York, 1959.

Lubin, B., E. Levitt and M. Zuckerman. Some personality differences between responders and nonresponders to a survey questionnaire. *J. Consult. Psychol.*, 1962, *26*, 192.

Mann, J. Self-ratings and the EPPS. *J. Appl. Psychol.*, 1958, *42*, 267-268.

Massy, W.F., A stochastic evolutionary adoption model for evaluating new products. Presented at the U.S. Meeting of TIMS, Boston, Mass. April, 1967.

—— Estimation of parameters for linear learning modes. Working Paper No. 78, Grad. Sch. Business, Stanford University, October, 1965.

—— Order and homogeneity of family specific MARKOV processes. *J. Mktg. Res.*, 1966, *e*, 85-88.

Massy, W.F. and R.E. Frank. Short term price and dealing effects in selected market segments. *J. Mktg. Res.*, 1965, *2*, 171-185.

——The study of consumer purchase sequences using factor analysis and simulation. *Proceedings* American Statistical Association, December 1964, 412-421 (b).

Massy, W.F., T.M. Lodahl and R.E. Frank. Collinearity in the Edwards Personal Preference Schedule, *J. Appl. Psych.*, 1966, *50*, 121-124.

Melikian, L.H. The relationship between Edwards' and McClelland's measures of achievement motivation. *J. Consult. Psychol.*, 1957, *22*, 296-298.

Montgomery, D.B., A probability diffusion model of dynamic market behavior. Unpublished Ph.D. Thesis at the Grad. Sch. of Bus., Stanford University, 1966.

Morrison, D.G. New models of consumer behavior: aids in setting and evaluating marketing plans. *Proceedings* Fall Conference Am. Mktg. Assoc., 1965, 323-337, (b).

—— *Stochastic Models for Time Series with Applications in Marketing.* Tech. Rep. 8, Jt. Prog. in Oper. Res. Stanford University, 1965. (a)

Murray, H.A. *Explorations in Personality.* New York: Oxford, 1938.

Mogar, R.E. Competition, achievement, and personality. *J. Counsel. Psychol.*, 1962, *9*, 168-172.

Newman, J.W. *Motivation Research and Marketing Management.* Boston: Harvard University, 1957.

Parzen, E. *Stochastic Processes.* San Francisco: Holden-Day, 1962.

Pessemier, E.A. and D.J. Tigert, Personality, activity and attitude predictors of consumer behavior. *Proceedings* Am. Mktg. Assoc., June, 1966.

Rice, W.T. Measurement of consumer loyalty: factor analysis as a market research tool. Unpublished M.S. Thesis, Mass. Inst. of Tech., 1962.

Ruch, D.M. Limitations of current approaches to understand buying behavior. In J.W. Newman, *On Knowing the Consumer,* New York: John Wiley, 1966.

Saltz, E., M. Reece and J. Ager. Studies of forced-choice methodology: individual differences in social desirability, *Educ. Psychol. Measmt.,* 1962, *22,* 365-370.

Shaw, M. Need achievement scales as predictors of academic success. *J. Educ. Psychol.,* 1961, *52,* 282-285.

Sheth, J.N. A behavioral and quantitative investigation of brand loyalty. Unpublished Ph.D. dissertation, University of Pittsburgh, 1960.

Smith, W.R. Product differentiation and market segmentation as alternative marketing strategies. *J. Mktg.,* 1956, *21,* 1-9.

Telser, L. Least square estimates of transition probabilities. In *Measurement in Economics.* Christ et al, Stanford University Press, 1963, 270-92.

Tolor, A. The relationship between insight and intraception. *J. Clin. Psychol.,* 1961, *17,* 188-189.

Tucker, W.T. The development of brand loyalty. *J. Mktg. Res.,* 1964, *1,* 32-35.

Wallis, W.A. and H.V. Roberts. *Statistics: A New Approach,* Glencoe, Ill. Free Press, 1956.

Westfall, R. Psychological factors in predicting product choice. *J. Mktg.,* 1962, *26,* 34-40.

Whyte, W.H., Jr. *The Organization Man.* New York: Simon & Schuster, 1956.

Worell, L. EPPS *n* achievement and verbal paired-associates learning. *J. Abnorm. Soc. Psychol.,* 1960, *60,* 147-150.

Zuckerman, M. The validity of the EPPS as a measure of dependency-rebelliousness. *J. Clin. Psychol.,* 1958, *14,* 379-382.

Zuckerman, M. and H. Goode. Suggestibility and dependency. *J. Consult. Psychol.,* 1958, *22,* 328.

INDEX

Table A-4
VARIABLE DICTIONARY FOR VALIDATION SAMPLE REGRESSIONS

A. Dependent Variables

Variable name	Reference table in text	Short description
ACTIV	2-9	Activity factor score (coffee and beer only)
UNITS	2-1	Number of units purchased
TRIPS	2-1	Number of shopping trips on which product was purchased
UNPTP	2-1	Average number of units purchased per trip
ATIVU	2-9	Activity in units factor score (tea only)
ATIVT	2-9	Activity in trips factor score (tea only)
LOYAL	2-9	General loyalty factor score
BRLOY	2-9	Brand loyalty factor score
BRAND	2-1	Number of different brands purchased
SHILB	2-1	Share of primary loyal brand
BCONS	2-9	Brand consistency (on 2nd and 3rd loyal-brands) factor score
SND1B	2-1	Standard normal deviate (for number of runs) for primary loyal brand
|SND1B|	–	Absolute value of SND1B
STLOY	2-9	Store loyalty factor score
STORE	2-1	Number of different stores in which product was purchased
SH1LS	2-1	Share of primary loyal store
PUNID	2-1[a]	Proportion of units purchased on a deal (coffee and tea only)
SND1S	2-1	Standard normal deviate (for number of users) for primary loyal store
|SND1S|	–	Absolute value of SND1S

B. Independent Variables: Personality[b]

DEFER	4-1,B-1	Deference, to get suggestions from others
ORDER	4-1,B-1	Order, to have things organized
EXHIB	4-1,B-1	Exhibition, to be the center of attention
AUTON	4-1,B-1	Autonomy, to be independent of others in making decisions
AFFIL	4-1,B-1	Affiliation, to be loyal to friends
INTRA	4-1,B-1	Intraception, to analyze one's motives and feelings
SUCCR	4-1,B-1	Succorance, to have others provide help when in trouble
ABASE	4-1,B-1	Abasement, to feel guilty when one does something wrong
NURTR	4-1,B-1	Nurturance, to help friends when they are in trouble
CHANG	4-1,B-1	Change, to experiment and try new things
ENDUR	4-1,B-1	Endurance, to keep at a job until it is finished
AGGRE	4-1,B-1	Aggression, to criticise others publicly

C. Independent Variables: Socio-economic and Demographic

WOMAGE	4-5	Age of wife
FAMSIZ	4-5	Size of family (number of members)
OWNCAR	4-5	Car ownership
MKTSIZ	4-5	Size of metropolitan area
INCOCC	4-6	Income-occupation transformed factor score

a Defined as "UNIDE/UNITS" (see text Table 2-1).
b Prefix "H" or "W" indicates husband's or wife's personality score.